Florida
FCAT
READING
COACH

GRADE
5

BY
STUART MARGULIES, PH.D.,
MARIA GOUDISS,
& VIVIENNE HODGES, PH.D.

EDUCATIONAL DESIGN

EDI 169

Acknowledgments

Excerpts from *A Shropshire Lad*, by A.E. Houseman, published in London by Kegan Pual, Trench, Treubner.

"Excerpt from "Still I Rise," from *And Still I Rise* by Maya Angelou. Copyright © 1978 by Maya Angelou, Reprinted by permission of Random House, Inc.

Excerpts from *Charlie and the Chocolate Factory* by Roald Dahl. Copyright © 1964 by Roald Dahl. Reprinted by permission of Alfred A. Knopf, Inc.

Excerpt from *Where the Red Fern Grows* by Wilson Rawls. Copyright © 1961 by Sophie S. Rawls, Trustee, or successor Trustee(s) of the Rawls Trust, dated July 31, 1991. Copyright © 1961 by The Curtis Publishing Company. Used by permission of Dell Books, a division of Bantam Doubleday Dell Publishing Group, Inc.

"El Poniente" by Ruth Comfort Mitchell, from *Narratives in Verse*, published by D. Appleton Company.

"Laughtertown" by Katherine Devereux Blake from *A Half-Century of Song, An Anthology of Hunter College Verse*.

"The Age of Jackson" adapted from *Our United States History* by Hilarie Staton. Copyright © 1996 Educational Design, Inc.

"The Strange Computer" by Shelley Fields. Reprinted by permission of the author.

"Water Safety" adapted from *The People's Medical Manual* by Howard and Martha Lewis, Doubleday & Co., 1986. Copyright © Clinical Communications, Inc. Reprinted by permission of the authors.

"The Grass on the Mountain" from *An Anthology of World Poetry*, edited by Mark Van Doren, Copyright © 1928 Literary Guild of America.

Florida FCAT Coach, Reading, Grade 5
EDI 169
0-87694-901-4

EVP, Publisher: Linda Sanford
VP, Editorial Director: Marie Spano
VP of Production: Dina Goren
VP, Creative Director: Rosanne Guararra
Art Director: Farzana Razak

Triumph Learning® 136 Madison Avenue, 7th Floor, New York, NY 10016
© 2000 Triumph Learning, LLC
A Haights Cross Communications, Inc. company

Table of Contents

Introduction to the Teacher

This book is aimed at the development of higher-order reading competencies by fifth-grade students. It prepares students for the **FCAT (Florida Comprehensive Assessment Test)** in Reading. The test taps students' reading comprehension strategies, as well as their ability to analyze different types of literature and synthesize information from a variety of sources.

The student reads a selection and then answers questions in a variety of formats: multiple choice, short answer, and extended response (Florida educators refer to these last two formats as "Read, Think, and Explain" Questions). *The FCAT Coach* begins by preparing students to answer questions in these three different formats. It teaches them the same criteria for answering written responses that the teachers who mark the **FCAT** are trained to measure.

Selections on the **FCAT** range from simple to difficult. The largest number of items require students to use their analytical skills and to compare and contrast different aspects of their reading material. The instructional strategies emphasized most heavily in *The FCAT Reading Coach* are aimed at developing the competencies tapped by these requirements.

Most teachers use *The Coach* by having their students proceed straight through the book. At the end, students take two practice tests, the first of which is followed (in the accompanying Teacher's Manual) by a lengthy discussion of answers. These tests not only provide review and practice, they also familiarize students with the format of the **FCAT**.

Another common way to use *The Coach* is to begin by giving students the first practice test. The teacher can use the results of this test to diagnose the areas requiring the most work. Some teachers only want a student to study those units in which he or she needs further work.

Selections included in this book match **FCAT** item profiles. They have been chosen for their high interest level. Students benefit most when they can read the stories at a relaxed pace and have plenty of time for classroom discussion.

We hope and expect not only that students will enhance their reading competencies and do better on the test, but that they will also enjoy the reading selections

Introduction to the Student

   This book, *The FCAT Reading Coach*, will help you to become a better reader. It will also help you do well on the **FCAT** by showing you how to answer the types of questions you will find on this test.

   At the end of the book are two Practice Tests. Both Practice Tests are like the **FCAT**. They will help you to do your best on the test.

Part I: FCAT Questions

Answering Different Kinds of Questions

There are three different kinds of **FCAT** questions:

◆ multiple-choice questions

◆ questions asking for short written answers

◆ questions asking for longer written answers

Multiple-Choice Items

When you answer multiple-choice questions, read the passage and then read the question very carefully. Look at the four choices and choose the answer you think is best. If you're not sure of the answer, reread the passage until you find the information that will allow you to answer the question.

There are always four answer choices. Even if you are not sure of the answer, always check off one of the choices. You will not lose any points if you make a guess.

Written Responses

The **FCAT** also asks questions which require either short or longer written answers. It calls these "Read, Think, and Explain" Questions.

A short written answer should be one or two sentences long, and never more than a paragraph. You can receive 0, 1, or 2 points for it. It should take you between three and five minutes to read a short answer question, plan your answer, and write it down.

Longer answers are several paragraphs long. They are worth 0, 1, 2, 3, or 4 points. They should take you about ten minutes to do.

The **FCAT** will tell you if your written answer should be short or long. This is how you will know.

Questions that require short written answers begin:

Questions that require longer written answers begin:

Strategies for Answering "Read, Think, and Explain" Questions

In this section you will read a story written by Shelley Fields. It is about a girl named Alison and a computer. Then you will learn some important rules for writing good answers.

Example 1

Alison didn't want to use the computer. "It's old and slow," she complained. The truth was that Alison didn't feel comfortable with computers, any computer.

"It's the only available computer," said her teacher, Mrs. Walsh, looking at her messy, handwritten report. "I want you to edit your report and then print it. You worked too hard on it to hand it in the way it looks."

Alison took her papers and went over to the computer Mrs. Walsh had set up in the back of the room. She looked at it with disgust. The computer was dusty. Not all the keys in the keyboard worked. It looked like it had been a long time since anyone had used it.

"Oh well," she muttered, "might as well make the most of it." She began typing her report about the size of planets that go around the sun. She began with a question, one that she didn't expect to find an answer to. "Who knows how many planets the size of the earth spin around a star the size of our sun?" Before Alison could type her next sentence, she felt the keys on her keyboard moving, it seemed, on their own. She looked at the monitor and saw these words:

"I DO. THERE ARE EXACTLY 4,234,222 PLANETS THE SIZE OF THE EARTH SPINNING AROUND 3,127,431 STARS THE SIZE OF OUR SUN IN THIS GALAXY."

"Whoa," shouted Alison, "there's something wrong with this computer."

Mrs. Walsh came rushing over. "What's the problem?" she asked.

"Check this out. I swear I didn't type in any numbers."

Mrs. Walsh folded her arms and stared down at Alison. She looked angry.

"What are you trying to pull, young lady? You have no idea if there are any planets the size of the earth, or any stars like ours, for that matter. Start your report all over again, and this time I want to see some facts and I want you to give me your sources, too. Don't waste any more of my time."

"What's with Miss Walsh today?" Alison typed, not daring to speak aloud.

"MRS. WALSH'S OLDEST SON IS VERY ILL TODAY. HE IS IN THE HOSPITAL," the computer responded.

A shiver ran down Alison's spine. That couldn't be true! What made those words appear on the monitor? She had to find out. Alison walked up to Mrs. Walsh's desk and cautiously brought up the subject of her son's health. "I hear he isn't well, Miss Walsh. Is that true? I'm so sorry if it is."

Mrs. Walsh's face filled with emotion. Then she smiled at Alison. "I don't know how you knew, but it's sweet of you to ask. We're very worried about him."

Now Alison knew there was something very unusual about the computer. She wondered what else the computer could tell her. "Will I get good grades in math?" "Where will we vacation next summer?" Bigger questions came to mind. "Will I be happy?" "Will I get married and have children?" "How old will I be when I die?" She didn't know which question to ask first.

Thoughtfully she approached the computer and typed in another question, her last. "What should I ask you, computer?"

The keys moved quickly and these words appeared on the monitor.

"IF YOU ARE WISE YOU WILL ASK NO MORE QUESTIONS. SOME THINGS BEST REMAIN UNANSWERED."

Alison smiled. "This computer is smart," she said.

Stay on Target

To get a high score on "Read, Think, and Explain" questions, read the question carefully. Be sure that:

◆ you answer the question that is asked.

◆ you answer **all** parts of the question.

◆ you include details from the story.

Be sure that you do **NOT**:

◆ answer with just one or two words.

Suppose you were asked,

  What was strange about the computer? Use details and information from the article in your answer.

You might answer:

the messages

Now this answer is partly accurate. The messages were strange. But the question expects you to write a long answer. It asks you to include supporting information from the passage. You won't earn a top score if you answer with two words or a short phrase. Always remember to write in complete sentences.

Read how Imani and Kayla answered the question.

Imani's Answer:

The computer is strange. It is very old and it is dusty. Alison doesn't like to use computers. I like to play games on my computer.

There is a problem with this answer. Imani's response doesn't answer the question. Imani says the computer is strange, but doesn't say why. She also includes information that is not connected to the question. She says that she likes to play games on her computer. This has nothing to do with the question.

Kayla's Answer:

The computer does strange things. It writes messages that are the answers to Alison's questions. When Alison asked about Mrs. Walsh, and what was wrong with her, the computer told Alison that Mrs. Walsh's son was sick. The computer also knew how many planets the size of earth revolved around stars the size of our sun. These answers are things that no one would know. It seems like the computer knows everything.

This answer is much better. Kayla tells why the computer is strange. She answers the question. She also gives details from the passage to support her answer. She takes the information from the story.

Answer All Parts of the Question

Read another question about the story. Then see how Elise and Brandon answered the question.

Alison says, "There's something wrong with this computer." Why did she say that? Do Alison's feelings about the computer change at the end of the story? Use details and information from the article in your answer.

Elise's Answer:

Alison says that there is something wrong with the computer because it answers questions that no one person or computer could answer. For example, it answered the question she asked about the planets that spin around a star like our sun. These questions are about things that no one would know.

There is a problem with Elise's answer. The first part of the answer is fine. But she didn't answer the second part. Part of the question asks "Do Alison's feelings about the computer change at the end of the story? Elise didn't answer this part of the question.

Now look at Brandon's answer.

Brandon's Answer:

Alison says that there is something wrong with the computer because it doesn't act like a normal computer. It gives answers to questions that no one could know. For example, when Alison types, "What's with Miss Walsh today?" the computer answers that Mrs. Walsh's son is ill. The computer couldn't know that. That's when Alison says that there is something wrong with the computer. She realizes that the computer is strange. But by the end of the story Alison decides that the computer is smart. I think this is because when Alison asked questions about her life, the computer said it was better not to know some things.

Brandon's answer is very good. He has answered both parts of the question. He describes why Alison said there is something wrong with the computer. He also tells how Alison's feelings changed at the end of the story. His answer was on target.

Use Details from the Story

Study the question and decide on your answer. Choose the main points you want to make. Then find details that support these points.

Be sure that:

◆ you support your answer with details and information from the passage.

◆ you don't include information not related to the passage. This won't help you to do well.

◆ you use information that is clear, on target, and accurate.

This next question is just like the kind of question you will find on the **FCAT**. Read how Jose and Emily answered it.

  What would be a good title for this story? Use details and information from the article to support your choice.

Jose's Answer:

"A Computer Answers Questions" is a good title for this story. I liked the part of the story where Alison asks Mrs. Walsh about her son. Mrs. Walsh felt sad about her son who was sick in the hospital. It was nice of Alison to ask her. I remember when I was in the hospital. I didn't like it at all.

Jose suggests a good title for the story, but he doesn't tell us why he has chosen it. He should have given us information about what happens when the computer answers questions. Jose tells us what he liked about the story. But he doesn't tell us why he chose his title. He doesn't support his answer. Jose also includes information that is not in the story. The people who grade the **FCAT** only want to know if you understood the story you read.

Here is Emily's answer.

Emily's Answer:

I would call this story "The Strangest Computer in the World" because the computer answers questions that no one would know the answer to. It knows everything. It knows that Mrs. Walsh's son is sick. It knows how many planets the size of the earth spin around a star the size of our sun in this galaxy.

This answer is very good. Emily chooses an excellent title for the story. Then she tells us why she chose this title. She gives us information from the story about why the computer is strange.

HELPFUL HINTS
FOR ANSWERING DIFFERENT KINDS OF QUESTIONS

1. For Multiple-Choice Questions:

◆ Make your best guess if you are unsure of the answer. Figure out which answers are definitely wrong and select the best remaining choice.

2. When answering "Read, Think, and Explain" questions:

◆ Read the question carefully. Be sure to answer the question that is asked.

◆ Remember to check back in the text.

◆ Answer all parts of the question.

◆ Include details from the story to support your answer.

◆ Stay on target. Do not include information that does not answer the question.

Selections for Practice

Read the passage below and then answer the four questions that follow. Two questions are of the multiple-choice type. The third question asks for a short answer. The final question requires a longer answer.

Selection 1

This selection is about a famous pilot. Someone who is a daredevil does things that can be dangerous.

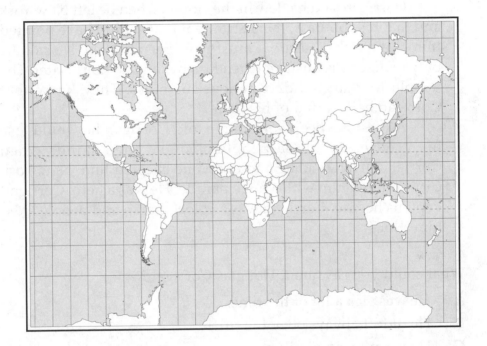

In 1938 Douglas Corrigan, a daredevil flier, surprised everyone when he landed his airplane in Dublin, Ireland. People were amazed because he had said that he was going to fly from New York to California. California is in a different direction from Dublin. People thought this was so strange that they gave him the nickname of "Wrong Way" Corrigan.

Corrigan had asked the people in charge of flights at that time to let him go from New York City to Europe. But the people in charge found out that his plane was in bad shape. So, they told Corrigan he couldn't go. The flight to Europe was over the Atlantic Ocean. This made the trip dangerous because if there was a problem with the plane, Corrigan wouldn't be able to land. Corrigan was told he could fly to California if he wanted to take a long flight. The trip to California was safer because it was over land the whole way. So Corrigan said he'd give up the transatlantic flight and go west to California.

Corrigan got into his plane, waved goodbye to the crowds, and took off. The crowds were surprised to see him go in the wrong direction, flying east toward Europe instead of west towards California. "Why did he go in the wrong direction?" people asked each other. When he arrived in Dublin he stepped out of his plane and said, "Just got in from New York. Where am I?"

Corrigan said he flew in the clouds when he left New York and that his compass, the instrument that should have pointed him in the right direction, must have been broken. He said he only realized his mistake when he saw land 28 hours later. The people in charge didn't believe his story. They knew that Corrigan had a mind of his own.

At first the people in charge told Corrigan he would lose his license. But these people changed their minds when Corrigan arrived home and everyone cheered him. New York City honored him with a huge parade. He was a hero. Corrigan kept his license. Corrigan was a colorful man and people liked him a lot.

 What could you say about Douglas Corrigan?

A. He was sick a lot of the time.

B. He didn't always obey the rules.

C. He wasn't a good pilot.

D. He wasn't very brave.

1B   Read these sentences from the passage.

> **The trip to California was safer because it was over land the whole way. So Corrigan said he'd give up the *transatlantic* flight and go west to California.**

What does *transatlantic* mean?

A.   across the Atlantic

B.   across the United States

C.   a train journey

D.   any trip across an ocean

1C   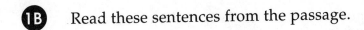 What happened when Corrigan returned to New York City? Use details and information from the article in your answer.

_____

_____

_____

_____

_____

_____

Douglas Corrigan got the nickname "Wrong-Way." Why did this happen? Use details and information from the article in your answer.

_____

_____

_____

_____

_____

_____

_____

_____

_____

_____

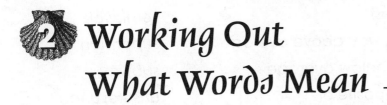

Part II: Reading

2 Working Out What Words Mean

Word Roots, Prefixes, and Suffixes

Many words are made up of prefixes, roots, and suffixes.

For example, let's look at the word coexistence. It's really made up of three parts:

PREFIX	ROOT	SUFFIX
co-	**exist**	**-ence**
co- is the prefix.	*exist* is the root .	*-ence* is the suffix.
It means "together."	It means "to be" or "to live."	It tells you that the word is a noun.

You should be able to figure out the meaning of a word formed in this way if you know the meaning of the root and the meaning of the prefix or suffix.

Here are some common **prefixes** with their meaning and an example of a word containing the prefix:

anti-	against	*antislavery*
bi-	two	*bicycle*
co-	together	*cooperate*
dis-	not	*disappointment*
in-	into or not	*input, inaccurate*
mid-	middle	*midflight*

multi-	many	*multipurpose*
mis-	wrong	*misuse*
pre-	before, ahead of time	*predate*
re-	back, again	*repaint*
semi-	half, part	*semicircle*
super-	above, way above average	*superman*
sub-	under, below average	*subway*
un-	not, opposite of	*unsure, undo*

Most **suffixes** tell you what part of speech a word is. Others have special meanings. Here are some:

-ful	full of, having a lot of	*peaceful*
-less	without, without power to do something	*helpless*
-like	like, similar to	*childlike*

Decide on the meaning of the word in the next example. The lists of prefixes will help you.

Example 1

 When is *midsummer*?

    A.   in August

    B.   in December

    C.   in May

    D.   in September

Choice A is correct. You know that mid- means "middle." If you join this prefix with the root summer you get "middle of the summer." From this it's easy to work out that midsummer is in August.

Example 2

2 What does *distrust* mean?

A.   feeling suspicious of others
B.   traveling a great distance
C.   feeling sick
D.   falling madly in love

 Your teacher will discuss your answer.

Multiple Meanings

Many common words have more than one meaning.

For example, the word *part* has a different meaning in each of these sentences:

> She took the largest *part* of the cake for herself.
> Tomorrow we must *part* for a month's vacation.
> I didn't get the *part* I wanted in the class play.
> My hairdresser changed my *part* to the other side of my head.

In the next example, you will read a sentence containing the word *grade*. Then you must decide which of the four answer choices uses the word grade in the same way.

Example 3

> **Emily was worried that she wouldn't get a passing *grade* in science.**

3 Which sentence uses the word *grade* in the same way as the sentence above?

    A. Diana had trouble driving because the *grade* of the road was very steep.

    B. What *grade* do you think you will get on your report?

    C. This *grade* of meat isn't good enough.

    D. When will you find out if Mrs. Wilbur's fourth *grade* class will go on the outing?

The sentence in the example uses the word grade to mean the mark a student receives in class. This is also how the word is used in Choice B.

Synonyms and Antonyms

SYNONYMS

Words that mean the same thing are called **synonyms** (the word is pronounced SIN-uh-nimz). The **FCAT** may show you a word and then ask you for a synonym. For example, you might read the word *dull* and have to choose a synonym from among:

    A. boring

    B. mean

    C. silly

    D. thin

Of course, the answer is Choice A, *boring*. The word boring is a synonym of *dull*. The other answer choices are not.

To do well on synonym questions, you usually have to already know what the words mean. If you don't know the meaning of a word, however, you may try this strategy:

See if you can change the word into one that has a slightly different form. For example, take the word *creations*. If you don't know the word, think of the similar word, *create*. You know that create means *to make*.

Now try this example:

Example 4

 Creations are

    A.   things bought at a candy store.

    B.   things someone made.

    C.   anything beautiful.

    D.   anything expensive.

 Your teacher will discuss your answer.

ANTONYMS

Words that have opposite meanings are called **antonyms**. For example, an antonym of *weak* is *strong*, an antonym of *tiny* is *large*, and an antonym of *wet* is *dry*.

Example 5

 An antonym of *tranquil* is

    A.   funny.

    B.   round.

    C.   noisy.

    D.   angry.

Choice C is correct. The word *tranquil* has the opposite meaning of noisy.

Using Context Clues

As you read, you may come across a word you don't know. You may be able to figure out what the word means by seeing how it is used. This is called "using context clues."

> The princess has lost her slipper.

What does the word *slipper* mean? Unless you already know the word, you can't work out its meaning from the sentence.

Now read this passage.

> The princess hurried out of the ballroom. She tripped as she ran down the staircase. After she jumped into the carriage, she looked down at her tiny foot. It was bare. The princess had lost her slipper.

If you read this passage carefully, you can figure out what slipper means. It is a type of shoe. The words and sentences around it help you to work out its meaning. You were able to figure out what slipper means from the context of the selection.

Read the next example and figure out the meaning of the word preference.

Example 6

Tonia likes to eat ice cream. She likes all kinds. But her *preference* is vanilla. No one else in the family picks vanilla. Both her sisters and her brother like chocolate more.

6   A *preference* is

    A.   a brother, a sister, or a cousin.

    B.   something that tastes good.

    C.   what you like best.

    D.   something that costs very little.

Choice C is the correct answer. If you read the sentences around the word *preference*, you can figure out that it means *liking something better*.

Phrases

Sometimes you must figure out what a phrase of two or more words means. Read the next example and work out the meaning of the phrase *hard of hearing*.

Example 7

Dan was very *hard of hearing*. Anita had to repeat everything Fred said to him so that Dan could understand.

7   Someone who is *hard of hearing*

    A.   likes to teach children

    B.   likes to talk a lot

    C.   can't stand people

    D.   can't hear very well

 Your teacher will discuss your answer.

HELPFUL HINTS
FOR WORKING OUT WHAT WORDS MEAN

1. Always check to see if you can divide a new word into *prefix*, *root*, and *suffix*. See if you can recognize the meaning of any part of the word. If so, find the answer choice that is closest to this meaning.

2. To figure out a word using *context clues*:

    ◆ Read the sentence with the new word.

    ◆ Read the sentences before and after this sentence.

    ◆ Take a guess at what the word probably means.

    ◆ Look at the answer choices. Pick the choice closest to your guess.

Selections for Practice

Selection 1

Jeff threw the ball into the air. It went up very high. The next time he threw it, the ball went towards the window. Everyone heard a large crash. The window *cracked into splinters*.

1 Something that has *cracked into splinters* is

A. heavy
B. broken
C. colorful
D. easy to see through

Selection 2

It was Jonnie's first day in class. When the teacher introduced him, he couldn't say a thing. He just looked down at his feet. At lunch time, Teresa and Henry came over to say hello, but Jonnie was *bashful*. He didn't say anything. He didn't know what to do.

2 Who else would be *bashful*?

A. someone who likes to make jokes and play pranks a lot
B. someone who enjoys giving speeches
C. someone who wants to help the teacher
D. someone who is frightened of talking to new people

Selection 3

Briana saw the sign in the window. She was sure that it said that the roller blades were on sale. But later, after she went back to the store, she realized she had *misunderstood* the sign. The roller blades were selling at their regular price.

3 Using your knowledge of prefixes, decide which of the following is a synonym of *misunderstood*.

A. wanted something very much

B. confused

C. was tired

D. won

Selection 4

4 An antonym of *strong* is

A. old.

B. powerful.

C. calm.

D. weak.

Selection 5

Rushan and Celeste went for a *spin* in their new convertible.

5 In which sentence does the word *spin* have the same meaning as in the sentence above?

A. Sue told Howie how much she'd enjoyed her *spin* around town.

B. A spider will *spin* a web in any corner of the room.

C. In early America, many women learned to *spin* wool to make clothes.

D. She watched him *spin* rapidly on his heels and walk away.

3 Finding the Main Idea and the Details That Support It

In this chapter, you will learn to identify a story's **main idea**. The main idea is what a story is mostly about. It is what you would come up with if you were asked to summarize a story in a single sentence.

Read the next passage. What is it mostly about?

Example 1

The okapi is an animal that looks a little like a giraffe. It has a very unusual tongue—14 inches long. The okapi's tongue is so long that it can wash its own ears. It can flick its tongue out and eat the top of shrubs and grasses.

1 The main idea is

- **A.** the okapi eats shrubs
- **B.** the okapi has a strange tongue
- **C.** the okapi looks a little like a giraffe
- **D.** the okapi washes its ears

The correct answer is B. The author tells us that the okapi has a very unusual tongue.

In the next example, the author talks about Sherlock Holmes and other famous characters. Try to figure out what the main idea is. When you answer the question, look carefully at the answer choices. They all sound like main ideas. Decide which main idea best sums up the passage.

Example 2

Perhaps the most popular character of all time in the mov ies and on television is Sherlock Homes. Sherlock Holmes is a detective. He is a character created a hundred years ago by the writer Sir Arthur Conan Doyle. There have been more than 200 movies about Sherlock Holmes.

Next to Sherlock Holmes, the most popular character in movies is Count Dracula. He is a monster who was also created about 100 years ago. And another monster, generally known as Frankenstein, has been portrayed in more than a hundred movies.

2 This selection mainly describes

A. the most popular movie and TV characters.

B. why Sir Arthur Conan Doyle created the character of Sherlock Holmes.

C. Sherlock Holmes as a detective.

D. how Count Dracula became a monster.

 Your teacher will discuss your answer.

On the **FCAT,** you may be asked simply, "What is the main idea of this story?" Or the question may be asked very differently. You could be asked, "What is the best title for the story?" or, "What is this story mostly about?" or, "What is the main topic of this story?"

Read Example 3 and answer the question.

Example 3

An alligator can shut its jaws with a tremendous snap. It smashes its teeth together with enough force to break a person's arm. But the muscles that open the jaw are weak. A child could hold the alligator's jaw closed. But the child had better not get tired and let the jaws get open. Once the jaws are open, the alligator can be very dangerous.

3 The best title for this selection is

A. "The Strength of an Alligator's Jaws"

B. "How to Hold an Alligator's Jaws Closed"

C. "Children and Animals"

D. "How an Alligator Eats"

 Your teacher will discuss your answer.

Theme

A **theme** is something the story teaches you.

There are thousands of possible themes. A story theme might be something like:

> Hard work pays off.

Or it might be:

> Never give up.

Usually the author doesn't tell you what the theme is. You have to figure it out.

Example 4

Uncle Samuel has a garden chair that is made of wood. Each spring he pulls it out of the shed. Each year he says that he has to paint it. "If I don't paint it, the wood will rot," he has told me every year. Then he puts it outside in the garden and we all use it. He never paints it.

This year he pulled the chair out of the shed and looked at it. "I guess I'd better paint it this year," he said. But when he picked it up the arm came off. The wood was rotted through.

 4 What lesson can the reader learn from this story?

A. Don't put off doing things until it is too late.

B. It's better not to buy wooden chairs or tables.

C. Some furniture doesn't last very long.

D. Chairs are hard to paint.

 Your teacher will discuss your answer.

Supporting Details

Besides the main idea, there are also details in a passage that support the main idea. These details help describe the main idea of a passage.

Passages and paragraphs often start with a main idea. Then the rest of the passage has details about that idea or examples of it.

The next example gives information about vaudeville shows. The first sentence is a good summary of the passage.

Example 5

Before the 1940's, and before there was television, vaude-ville shows were the most popular kind of light entertainment. A vaudeville show consisted of a series of live acts— song-and-dance acts, comic acts, and acrobatic acts. Many theaters offered a combination of a movie followed by a vaudeville show. Vaudeville was funny and light-hearted, and it earned a place in the hearts of millions of Americans. But by the late 1940's, the days of vaudeville began to come to an end.

5 The main idea is that vaudeville shows were the most popular kind of light entertainment before the 1940's. Which detail supports this main idea?

A. By the late 1940's, the days of vaudeville began to come to an end.
B. Theaters offered a combination of a movie and a vaudeville show.
C. Vaudeville earned a place in the hearts of millions of Americans.
D. A vaudeville show consisted of live acts.

The correct choice is C. This detail supports the main idea. It gives more information about the main idea.

Sequence

The **FCAT** may ask you questions about what happened first or last.

Key words like *before* and *after*, or *first* and *last*, help you to understand the order in which things happened. We call the order in which things happen their **sequence**.

Read the next example and decide what occurred last.

Example 6

First Geraldo pulled out the clutch lever and pushed the driving lever to START. Next he pulled the cord to start the engine. Finally, after the engine was going, he pushed in the clutch lever and put the driving lever at FULL. Now he was ready to mow the lawn.

6 When did Geraldo pull out the clutch lever?

  A. after pushing the driver lever on FULL
  B. after he started the engine
  C. before he pulled the cord
  D. while mowing the lawn

 Your teacher will discuss your answer.

Some selections have a clear sequence of events, even though they do not use key words. In cases like these, you can usually work out the sequence by reading carefully and looking for clues. Some possible clues are the time of day, calendar dates, or ages.

Read Example 7 and decide on the correct order of events.

Example 7

Salvador left the gym at around 4 in the afternoon. He went home and spent some time practicing his drums. After dinner, he did his homework. It wasn't until the next morning that he realized his watch was missing. The watch was a present from his grandmother, and Salvador had no idea what he had done with it. He was really upset.

When he got to school, he went immediately to the Lost and Found, but no one had brought in a watch. He looked through his backpack more carefully, taking everything out of it. But it wasn't there. He went through his locker item by item, but nothing turned up. He told all his friends, and he put up notices promising a reward. By the end of the day, he was so upset he didn't know what he would do.

It was now 3:30. Salvador went to the gym. No one there had seen the watch. He was really depressed. He went into the locker room, and tried to remember which locker he had used the day before. Was it 105 or 107? He wasn't sure. He looked in 105. Nothing was there. He looked in 107. There, on top, his eye caught the reflection of something shiny. He reached up and touched it. It was the watch. He nearly cried with joy.

7 READ THINK EXPLAIN What happened immediately after Salvador went to the Lost and Found?

_____

_____

_____

_____

_____

_____

The correct answer is that he looked through his backpack more carefully and he went through his locker item by item.

HELPFUL HINTS
FOR FINDING THE MAIN IDEA
AND THE DETAILS THAT SUPPORT IT

1. After you read a selection, ask, "What was the story about?" Try to sum up your answer in a single sentence. This is the *main idea*.

2. Don't confuse a story detail with the main idea. Details help tell you about the main idea.

3. Look out for a "lesson for life" that the story teaches. This "lesson for life" is the *theme* or message of the story.

4. Make sure that the theme is one that the story teaches. Don't choose a theme that sounds good but has nothing to do with the actual story.

5. To decide the order in which things happen, look out for key words like *first, last, before,* and *after.* If there are no key words, find the sentence with the event described in the question. Then read the sentences before and after this sentence.

Selections for Practice

Selection 1

Sara Winchester built the strangest house ever seen. Every year she added more rooms. Some rooms were only a few inches wide. Some rooms were big enough for a king.

Some rooms had staircases which didn't go anywhere. The staircase would just stop at the ceiling. Some rooms had windows which opened onto a plain wall. You couldn't see anything out of these windows.

Mrs. Winchester was very rich. She thought she would die unless she kept adding rooms to her house. She hired carpenters to keep building new rooms. They worked for her for 38 years. It must have been a weird job to keep adding rooms to the same house for 38 years.

The house cost five million dollars. There is no other house at all like it anywhere.

1 A good title for this passage is

A. "Staircases That Go Nowhere"
B. "Mrs. Winchester's Strange House"
C. "An Expensive House"
D. "Rooms Big Enough for a King"

Selection 2

Great actors and actresses usually find a lot of roles on television, in the movies, or on the stage. The others have a tough time getting work. It is hard to be a success in acting. Only the best people get jobs.

But the Cherry sisters were different. The Cherry sisters weren't great. They weren't good. They were terrible. People said they were the worst actresses anyone had ever seen.

But they were very successful. Everyone heard about how bad they were. Everyone wanted to see really bad actors. They were so popular that all their shows were sold out.

The audience laughed at them because they acted so poorly. People would get up and throw tomatoes at them. The four Cherry sisters bought an iron fence. They put it on the stage before each show. The fence protected them from the vegetables the audience threw at the stage.

The Cherry Sisters spent 10 years traveling through America. The theaters they played in were always packed. Then the sisters retired. They were all rich.

Everyone knew the sisters were awful, but no one ever told these four ladies that they couldn't act. All four thought they were great actresses.

2 What lesson does this story teach?

A. Learning to protect yourself is important.

B. Things don't always happen the way you think they will.

C. If you are good at what you do you will always succeed.

D. It's hard to do two things at once.

Selection 3

Most people who catch the flu are sick for a few days and then recover. But some flus are very serious. Millions of people died from the flu epidemic at the end of World War I.

The flu is a virus. Animals also get ill from viruses. In 1872, before there were many cars, people traveled by horse. But one out of every four horses died that year from a virus. People couldn't get to work or travel anywhere because so many horses were dead.

3 This selection is mostly about viruses being dangerous to both people and animals. Which detail supports this main idea?

A. The flu lasts a few days.

B. The flu is a virus.

C. Animals get ill from viruses.

D. Some flus are serious.

Selection 4

All Gabrielle could ever see were shapes and colors. She could never focus clearly on anything. She couldn't see the difference between a basketball and softball. She had to touch them to see which was which. She spent a lot of time alone and she and her parents believed she could never enjoy any sport, except for swimming.

But when she was seven, doctors found a new operation to repair her eyes. Gabrielle, her family, and even her eye doctor, were surprised at this wonderful discovery. Within a few months, Gabrielle could see as well as anyone, and within a few years she was a star at track. She came in second at the State Championship.

Sometimes Gabrielle could hardly believe all this was happening to her. She now had a healthy body, many friends, and a sport she loved. Who could tell what would happen next?

4 What happened last?

A. Gabrielle was a great runner.

B. The eye doctor helped Gabrielle.

C. Gabrielle liked to swim a lot.

D. Gabrielle's eyes were very bad.

Selection 5

This passage comes from Charlie and the Chocolate Factory, a book written by Roald Dahl. Charlie's family is very poor and sometimes they do not have enough food to eat.

There is something about very cold weather that gives one an enormous appetite. Most of us find ourselves beginning to crave rich steaming stews and hot apple pies and all kinds of delicious warming dishes; and because we are all a great deal luckier than we realize, we usually get what we want— or near enough. But Charlie Bucket never got what he wanted because his family couldn't afford it, and as the cold weather went on and on, he became ravenously and desperately hungry. Both bars of candy, the birthday one and the one Grandpa Joe had bought, had long since been nibbled away, and all he got now were those thin cabbagy meals three times a day.

Then all at once, the meals became even thinner.

The reason for this was that the toothpaste factory, the place where Mr. Bucket worked, suddenly went bust and had to close down. Quickly, Mr. Bucket tried to get another job. But he had no luck. In the end, the only way in which he managed to earn a few pennies was by shoveling snow in the streets. But it wasn't enough to buy even a quarter of the food that seven people needed. The situation became desperate. Breakfast was a single slice of bread for each person now, and lunch was maybe half a boiled potato.

Slowly but surely, everybody in the house began to starve.

And every day, little Charlie Bucket, trudging through the snow on his way to school, would have to pass Mr. Willy Wonka's giant chocolate factory. And every day, as he came near to it, he would lift his small pointed nose high in the air and sniff the wonderful sweet smell of melting chocolate. Sometimes, he would stand motionless outside the gates for several minutes on end, taking deep swallowing breaths as though he were trying to eat the smell itself.

5A The main idea is that Charlie is hungry. Which detail supports this main idea?

    A.   Mr. Bucket tried to get another job.

    B.   Breakfast was a single slice of bread.

    C.   Charlie Bucket trudged through snow to school.

    D.   Very cold weather gives you an enormous appetite.

5B What does Charlie do when he passes the chocolate factory? Why does he act this way? Use details and information from the passage in your answer.

41

4 Finding the Author's Purpose

Authors have their own reasons in mind when they write. They may want to teach or inform their readers, persuade readers to agree with them, make their readers laugh, or convey a particular mood.

Understanding the **author's purpose** helps us to understand what we are reading.

Read Example 1 and decide on the purpose of this passage.

Example 1

> After you finish the test, be sure to put the exam on the front desk and return your answer sheet to the attendant. Then you may leave.

1 Why do you think the author wrote the lines printed above?

A. to amuse readers with jokes about tests
B. to tell readers what to do after they finish the test
C. to persuade readers that the test matters a lot
D. to explain why it is important to finish the test

These lines are instructions about what to do when you finish a test. Choice B is correct. The lines aren't funny. They don't try to persuade readers. And they don't explain why it is important to finish the test. They simply tell readers what to do.

Authors have many ways of getting their points across. The language they choose has an effect on you and may make you feel a particular way.

Read Example 2. What is the mood of this poem? How does it make you feel? How does the boy in the poem feel? How does his mother feel?

Example 2

Many children believe that Santa Claus flies through the air and brings them toys at Christmas. But one day parents tell their sons and daughters that Santa Claus is not real. In this poem a mother tells her eight-year-old son the truth about Santa Claus.

EIGHTH BIRTHDAY

by Donald A. Cook

When mother said
"I should tell you now the truth
about Santa Claus,"
My throat went dry and
My legs began to tremble.
I thought why all this fear?
Haven't you been ready, ready?
But then I saw the reason:
My poor mother crying,
And she could not stop.

2 How does the poet show that the boy was afraid?

A. The boy's throat was dry and his legs shook.

B. The boy told his mother he was ready to hear the truth.

C. The boy started to cry and he couldn't stop.

D. The boy didn't say anything.

 Your teacher will discuss your answer.

Persuasion

Writers often hope to persuade us to agree with them. Newspapers are filled with articles, called editorials, that try to make us change our minds and agree with their writers. Letters-to-the-Editors are also written by people who have strong opinions. The next example is a Letter-to-the-Editor from a local newspaper. Decide what the author wants his readers to think after they read it.

Example 3

Dear Editor:

The state government has announced that it will increase the amount of tax we pay when we buy an automobile.

I say, enough! The state is out of control! It's bad enough that we are already taxed more than any other state, but putting an additional tax on cars is unforgivable.

Fewer people will be able to buy new cars. The people who make cars and the people who sell cars will lose their jobs. We must let state leaders know that we are strongly opposed to this proposal. Write your legislators today.

Sincerely yours,
Terry Wolffe

  Why did Terry Wolffe write this letter? What opinions did he express? Use details and information for the article to explain your answer.

_____

_____

_____

_____

_____

_____

Terry Wolffe is clearly against increasing taxes on cars. And he gives reasons why he is against this proposal, such as fewer people being able to afford new cars, and jobs being lost. We can guess that the author hopes to persuade his readers to agree with him.

When you have to answer a question about the author's purpose, be sure that you provide details to support your answer. You will not get full marks on the **FCAT** if you answer simply "to persuade" or "to inform."

HELPFUL HINTS
FOR FINDING THE AUTHOR'S PURPOSE

---

1. Where you read a selection can give you an important clue about the author's purpose. Newspaper editorials usually try to persuade. School texts try to instruct or inform.

2. It may help if you know who the author is. Funny writers, for example, probably want to amuse you and make you laugh.

3. Some writing styles have a special effect on readers. For example, short, snappy sentences can create a sense of drama and make you feel tense.

Selections for Practice

Selection 1

Jasper watched as his team scored the winning run. He jumped in the air and shouted and cheered himself hoarse. This would mean that they had a chance at the title. He couldn't believe they had come back from so far behind. Jason smiled to himself all the way home.

1 What is the mood is expressed by the author of this selection?

A. happiness

B. anger

C. sadness

D. boredom

Selection 2

What is the best thing to do if you smell smoke?

First of all, don't panic. Feel your door to see if it is warm. If so, call 911 and tell them there is a fire and you are trapped in your apartment. If the door is not warm to the touch, open it carefully and walk into the corridor. Do not take the elevator. Use the stairs to reach the ground floor.

2 The author wrote this to

A. explain what to do if there is a fire.

B. instruct people on the dangers of fire.

C. list the different kinds of fires.

D. describe how fires get started.

Selection 3

Most inventors don't make any money for their work. For example, Peter Cooper thought of the idea of Jell-O. He didn't make any money from it because people didn't like Jell-O at first. It took many years before it became popular. And by then, Peter Cooper had sold the idea for a very small amount of money. When Jell-O did become popular, the new owner became very rich. None of the millions went to the real inventor, Peter Cooper.

3 READ THINK EXPLAIN Why do you think the author wrote this article about inventors? Tell why you think this.

_____

_____

_____

_____

_____

_____

5 Finding, Understanding, and Organizing Information _____

Researching Information

Information can be found in many different places. Your school texts contain information about math, science, and social studies. Up-to-date information can be found in newspapers and magazines. Reference books like dictionaries and encyclopedias, can be very helpful if you have to write a paper.

These information sources are mostly in printed form. But today a great deal of information is stored on computers. You might also be able to obtain information that is contained on video or film.

Your school library has information in book form and stored on computers. Some of your school computers can probably connect to the Internet. In the years to come, we will find more and more knowledge on the Internet.

Useful reference books include:

- **Atlases**   Collections of maps and other geographical in
                       formation. Road atlases provide road maps of a
                       specific area.

- **Encyclopedias**   Provide information about the whole range of
                       knowledge; some encyclopedias deal only with
                       a particular field.

- **Dictionaries**   Tell us what words mean, and how to spell and
                       pronounce them.

Now read what the dictionary has to say about the word order:

or • der *noun* 1. The way things are arranged or placed. 2. A command telling people what to do. 3. A request to buy something. 4. A group of related animals or plants. [<Latin *ordo*].

The dictionary tells you what part of speech the word *order* is—it is a noun. It tells you which language the word comes from. You also learn that a word can have several different meanings.

Now answer a question about the word *order*.

Example 1

The captain *ordered* his troops to march doubletime.

 You read four different meanings of the noun order. Which means having a captain tell his troops to march *doubletime*?

    A.   Meaning 1

    B.   Meaning 2

    C.   Meaning 3

    D.   Meaning 4

 Your teacher will discuss your answer

Finding Information Within a Text

Now suppose your teacher has asked you to write a paper about honeybees and what they eat.

Example 2

2A Which of the following resources might give you more information about honeybees and what they eat?

    A.   a dictionary

    B.   a general encyclopedia

    C.   an almanac

    D.   a world atlas

The correct answer is Choice B. You read that encyclopedias contain information about a wide range of topics, including scientific ones.

Now answer a different kind of question about using sources.

Which of the following books would be most likely to give more information about honeybees?

    A.   "Poisonous Snakes of South America"

    B.   "Monkeys of Africa"

    C.   "The Age of Dinosaurs"

    D.   "Flying Insects"

 Your teacher will discuss your answer.

Now suppose your teacher has asked you to write a paper about snakes. You ask your school librarian where you can find books on snakes. She shows you a shelf full of books. You pick one up and look at its Table of Contents.

A **table of contents** is a list of the chapters in a book. It also shows the page on which each chapter begins. Look at the table of contents from a book about snakes and answer the following question.

Example 3

Introduction	ix
1. Snakes of the Woods	1
2. Water Snakes	11
3. Poisonous Snakes	19
4. Desert Snakes	26
5. Snake Skin Types	39
6. How to Handle a Snake	43

If you wanted to read about dangerous snakes, which chapter would you read?

A. Chapter 1
B. Chapter 3
C. Chapter 5
D. Chapter 6

The correct answer is B. Chapter 3 describes poisonous snakes. Poisonous snakes are dangerous.

 Look at the Table of Contents again. If you wished to read about different kinds of snake skins, which pages would you read?

A. pages 1-10
B. pages 11-18
C. pages 26-38
D. pages 39-42

 Your teacher will discuss your answer.

Another way to find out what is in a book is to look at its **index**. On the following page, you will find part of the index from a book about Florida.

You see three main items in this index. In alphabetical order they are: Early Settlements, Recreation and Places of Interest, and Regions. Listed below these items are the pages where you can find this information. For example, you can read about coral reefs in Biscayne National Park on page 27.

Now answer a question about the index.

Example 4

4 Which two topics can you read about on page 28?

_____

_____

_____

_____

_____

 Your teacher will discuss your answer.

Interpreting Graphics

PICTURES

Have you ever heard the saying, "A picture is worth 1,000 words"? Pictures, graphs, and maps can often help you to make sense out of what you read. Here is an example:

Example 5

Artie and Arlene had front row seats at the concert. They loved the music. They clapped so hard at the end of the performance that their palms hurt. All the way home, they talked about the group, and how well they had performed. They loved the singer's voice, and the guitarist and the trumpet player were outstanding. So much sound for a group of five people!

5 The picture tells you something that you could not know from reading the paragraph. The picture tells you that

A.   the singer was a woman.

B.   there was a guitarist in the band.

C.   there were five people in the band.

D.   there was a pianist.

The correct answer is A. The picture shows a woman singing. This is the only way you could know the answer to the question. All the other information is in the passage.

MAPS

Maps help you find your way. They can tell you about the entire world. If you're looking at a map, the map compass—sometimes called a "compass rose"—helps you find which direction is east, west, north, or south. The map key tells you what the different symbols on a map stand for.

In the next example, you will see a map of a town called Willistown. Study it and answer the question.

Example 6

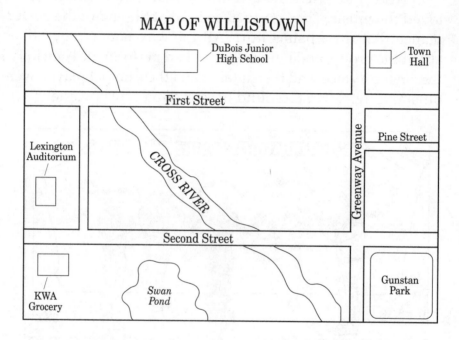

MAP OF WILLISTOWN

6 If you were to travel from the Town Hall to Gunstan Park, which route would you take?

A. First Street

B. Second Street

C. Greenway Avenue

D. Prince Andrew Lane

 Your teacher will discuss your answer.

Combining Text and Graphics

Some **FCAT** questions ask you to look at two graphic elements, or at a graphic and an article. You must use information from both sources when you answer the question.

In Example 7 you will read a short passage and then look at a drawing.

Example 7

Woodland Indians usually built their homes with the wood that grew so plentifully all around them. The tribes that lived in the north built houses with thick walls— those in the south left the side open to the breezes. Many of the people who lived in the east built longhouses like the one below, where several families lived. In most longhouses, each family built its own fire for cooking and keeping warm.

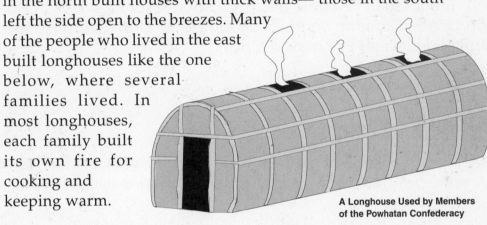

A Longhouse Used by Members of the Powhatan Confederacy

7 READ THINK EXPLAIN How many families lived in this longhouse? How can you tell? Use details and information from both the diagram and the text?

_____

_____

_____

_____

_____

 Your teacher will discuss your answer.

Organizing Information

By using reference books, such as encyclopedias, and by looking at maps and graphs, you are gathering information. When you have finished gathering your information, you must organize it so that it is easier to use.

TABLES AND LISTS

One good way of organizing information is to put it into a table. Some information is easier to understand when it is in a table than when it is written in sentences.

The table in Example 8 tells you about some events in Florida's history. The first column contains dates. The second column tells you about significant events in Florida's history.

Example 8

1853	University of Florida founded at Gainesville.
1860	Florida Railroad crosses state, Fernandina to Cedar Keys.
1881	Florida sells 4 million acres of land to developers.
1889	Lue Gim Gong develops a new variety of orange.
1895	Severe freeze almost destroys citrus crops.
1907	Draining operations begun in the Everglades.
1925-26	Land boom brings flood of settlers.
1938	Overseas Highway to Key West completed.
1947	Everglades National Park created.
1954	Sunshine Skyway across Tampa Bay opened.
1962	First astronauts orbited earth after leaving from Cape Canaveral.

8 When did Florida start selling large amounts of land?

    A. 1853

    B. 1881

    C. 1947

    D. 1962

The correct answer is Choice B. This was the year that Florida sold 4 million acres of land to developers.

GRAPHS AND CHARTS

Graphs and charts are also a good way of handling information, particularly information with a lot of numbers.

Suppose you read a poll about popular food: 12,413 people liked pizza, 3,234 liked tacos, 8,101 preferred hot dogs, and 12,512 liked hamburgers. It's hard to remember all these figures and organize them in your mind.

Below you see this same information in a pie chart. It shows the most popular foods. Each slice of the pie represents a different food.

Example 9

9 Which is the LEAST popular?

    A. hamburgers

    B. hotdogs

    C. pizza

    D. tacos

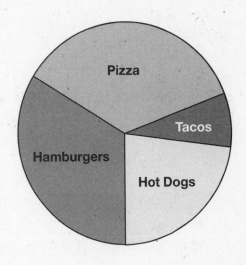

 Your teacher will discuss your answer.

HELPFUL HINTS
FOR FINDING, UNDERSTANDING,
AND ORGANIZING INFORMATION

1. Here are some useful reference books:

   ◆ *Encyclopedias* tell you about a wide range of information.

   ◆ *Atlases* have maps of the whole world or of just one area.

   ◆ *Dictionaries* provide lists of words and their meanings.

2. *Tables of contents* and *indexes* let you know if a book contains the information you want and help you to find it.

3. Look carefully at the title and labels on *maps*, *graphs*, and *charts*.

   ◆ Graphs often have numbers at the bottom or along the side. Be sure you understand what the numbers stand for.

   ◆ Map keys tell you the meaning of symbols used in the map. Map scales tell you how far apart places on a map are.

Selections for Practice

Selection 1

> **deal** *noun* 1. The distribution of playing cards. 2. A bargain. 3. A business agreement. 4. (Slang) An important issue. — *verb* 5. To give someone his share. 6. To do business with. [< Old English *delen* to divide]

1 Bringing you home was no big *deal*.

Which meaning of the word *deal* was used in the sentence above?

- A. noun, meaning 1
- B. noun, meaning 4
- C. verb, meaning 5
- D. verb, meaning 6

Selection 2

CHAPTER 1: Bringing Home a Puppy	1
CHAPTER 2: Training and Obedience	4
CHAPTER 3: Favorite Breeds	15
American Cocker Spaniels	15
German Shepherds	17
Irish Setters	19
Labrador Retrievers	21
Poodles	23
CHAPTER 4: Food and Exercise	28
CHAPTER 5: Grooming	36

 Which chapter would you read to find out how to teach your dog to "sit"?

- A. Chapter 1
- B. Chapter 2
- C. Chapter 4
- D. Chapter 6

2B Which pages of Chapter 3 would tell you about Irish setters?

A. 15-16

B. 17-18

C. 19-20

D. 23-25

Selection 3

Look carefully at the map. It shows how the land in the United States is used. The map contains many symbols. On the left of the map is a key. It shows you what the map symbols mean.

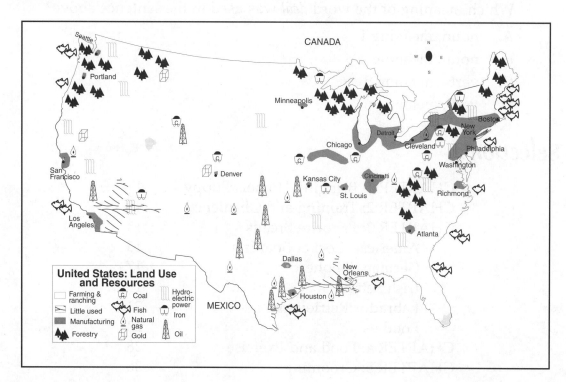

3A Which city is surrounded by oil wells?

A. Atlanta

B. Houston

C. Portland

D. Richmond

3B What do the cities on the coasts have in common?

    A. They have no forests.

    B. They have no natural gas.

    C. They have a big mining industry.

    D. They have a big fishing industry.

Selection 4

The police keep computer drawings of criminals wearing disguises to help train new officers. These two drawings show a criminal before and after he disguised himself.

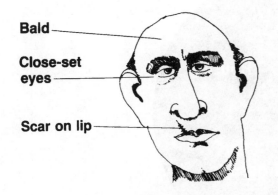

1. Original Drawing of Criminal

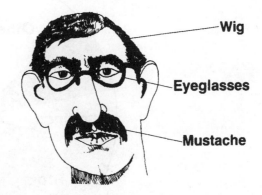

2. Drawing of Criminal in Disguise

4   How do criminals try to make themselves look different? What parts of the face do they disguise? Use details and information from the drawings in your answer.

_____

_____

_____

_____

_____

_____

Selection 5

Latisha Thompson loved shoes. She wore a different pair of shoes to work every day of the year. That was easy for her to do because she owned more than 1,000 pairs of shoes. Latisha spent more money on shoes than she did on her car or her house.

But most other Americans don't spend as much on clothing. Look at the pie chart below to decide how most families spend their money.

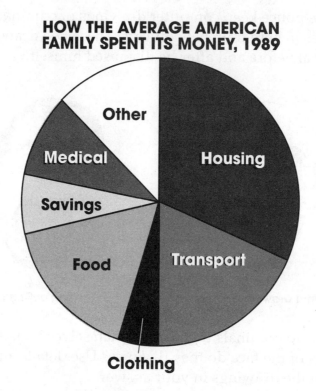

HOW THE AVERAGE AMERICAN FAMILY SPENT ITS MONEY, 1989

5 Which item cost most for the average family in 1989?

   A. food

   B. transport

   C. housing

   D. shoes and clothing

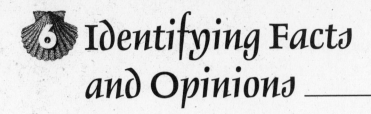 Identifying Facts and Opinions

A **fact** is something you can check. You can find out if it is true.

An **opinion** is based on feelings. It is a statement that some people might not agree with. Even a statement that almost everyone would agree with, like "It's nice to be happy," is an opinion.

When statements are supported by such adjectives as *wonderful*, *kind*, *caring*, or *mean*, it is usually pretty hard to find out for sure if the claims being made are true. Such statements are likely to be opinions.

Here are examples of some facts and opinions:

Facts	Opinions
Jackie has red hair.	Jackie is friendly.
Lincoln was our 16th President.	Lincoln was our smartest President.
I went surfing last week.	The waves were perfect for surfing.
Jill went to see the Marlins.	The Marlins are a great team.

Read the following sentences and decide which ones can be proven (facts) and which ones are based on feelings (opinions).

Write **F** if it's a fact.

Write **O** if it's an opinion.

____ Washington was a good President.

____ Angela has green eyes.

____ Therese-Anne's birthday is Wednesday.

 Your teacher will discuss your answer.

Read Example 1.

Decide which statements are facts and which are opinions.

Example 1

Richard and Chuck went camping last weekend. They saw several wild animals, including a raccoon and a fox. The weather was terrible. It rained every evening. Their tent wasn't very good either.

1 | READ THINK EXPLAIN | Pick out one fact from the sentences above. Then pick out one opinion.

_____

_____

_____

_____

_____

_____

Three of the sentences in the passage contain facts. They can be checked. You can check whether or not Richard and Chuck went camping, whether they saw wild animals, and whether it rained every night.

But you can't prove whether the statement that the weather was terrible is fact. Someone may disagree, even though it rained every evening. That statement is an opinion. The last sentence also contains an opinon.

The **FCAT** may ask you to explain why a statement in the text is a fact or an opinion.

Example 2

It was December 6, 1877. A group of America's greatest scientists were listening. What they heard was:

Mary had a little lamb
His fleece was white as snow

These scientists were listening to the first record ever made. Thomas Edison had worked many years to produce this first recorded song. He made the record to prove his new invention really worked. One scientist said that the song of Mary and her lamb was the sweetest song in the world.

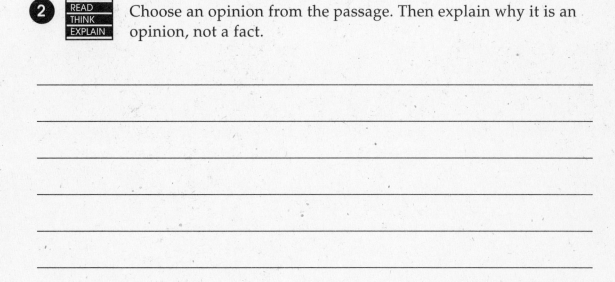 **2** READ THINK EXPLAIN — Choose an opinion from the passage. Then explain why it is an opinion, not a fact.

_____

_____

_____

_____

_____

_____

There is only one opinion in this passage—the scientist's opinion that the song of Mary and her lamb was the sweetest song in the world. This sentence contains a word—sweetest—that warns you that you are probably dealing with an opinion. Remember that opinions often include such words as *sweet* or *nice*, or *good* and *bad*.

The question asked you to explain why the sentence you chose is an opinion. Opinions can't be proved. You cannot prove that the song was the sweetest song in the world. The scientist may have felt that it was the sweetest song in the world. But you cannot prove it. It was his opinion only.

HELPFUL HINTS
FOR IDENTIFYING FACTS AND OPINIONS

1. To spot *facts* (as opposed to opinions), ask yourself: Can this statement be checked or proved? If so, it is a fact.

2. Here are some ways to spot *opinions*:

   Ask: Does this statement show what the writer feels? If so, it is an opinion.

   Ask: Does this statement have words that show feelings, such as love or fear or hope? Does it have words like good or bad? If so, it is probably an opinion.

Selections for Practice

Selection 1

A translator must speak at least two languages. A person who speaks French and English can translate from one language to another. Some people speak three or four or even ten languages. Such people are great translators. But George Schmidt is beyond comparison. Born in 1901, he worked at the United Nations as a translator. He can translate in 66 languages. He is also one of the world's most interesting people.

1 **READ THINK EXPLAIN** Pick out one FACT from the sentences above. Then pick one OPINION.

_____

_____

_____

_____

_____

Selection 2

The praying mantis usually feeds on other insects. But, if hungry, it will eat its own relatives. The praying mantis is so vicious that people in some parts of the world use it as a guard to keep other insects away. A string is tied around its leg. The string is then tied to the bedpost. Insects that come near the bed at night become the midnight snack of the praying mantis. Because it eats insects, the praying mantis is helpful to farmers.

  Choose a FACT from this passage.
Then explain why it is a fact, not an opinion.

_____

_____

_____

_____

_____

_____

Selection 3

Spies try to carry messages. They have many tricks to avoid getting caught. This selection tells about one spy who was never caught.

There have been many great spies. A man named Richeborg was among the best. He was a dwarf, one of the shortest dwarfs who ever lived. He was brave and intelligent, but so are many spies. His great trick was to dress as a child. He behaved like a little boy. No one ever searched him. He looked too young to be a spy. He carried messages across the borders without ever being searched.

Choose an OPINION from this passage.
Then explain why it is an opinion, not a fact.

_____

_____

_____

_____

_____

_____

Deciding How Things Are Alike And How They Are Different

Using Graphic Organizers to Compare and Contrast

Graphic organizers can help you compare and contrast people, things, or ideas. There are many different types of graphic organizers which can be used in a variety of ways.

Suppose, for example, that you were asked to compare a basketball game to a baseball game. You could draw two columns like the ones below, one headed by the word "Basketball" and the other by the word "Baseball." This chart will help you organize your information. The next step would be to decide how these two sports differ and then write these differences in the two columns.

BASKETBALL	BASEBALL
5 players on a team	9 players on a team
Game takes one hour of play	Game takes 9 innings

In the next example, you will read about two teachers. Then you will see a chart which lists the differences between them. Your task will be to complete this chart.

Example 1

Mr. Rizzo and his wife were both teachers. Mr. Rizzo taught fifth grade science. He liked to take his class on field trips and show them about the things they were studying in class. Mrs. Rizzo taught chemistry in high school. She spent a lot of time doing experiments with her students. Everyone enjoyed her labs. Mr. and Mrs. Rizzo were both very popular. They told a lot of jokes and knew everyone's name. On Saturdays Mr. Rizzo liked to go hiking. But he usually went alone because Mrs. Rizzo preferred relaxing on the couch reading science fiction stories.

1 How do Mr. and Mrs. Rizzo differ?

MR. RIZZO

_____

_____

_____

MRS. RIZZO

_____

_____

_____

Now look at how one student filled in the blanks.

MR. RIZZO

Taught fifth grade

Liked to hike

Took class on field trips

MRS. RIZZO

Taught in high school

Liked to read science fiction

Did experiments with students

There are many similarities between Mr. and Mrs. Rizzo. They are both teachers. They are both popular. But Mr. Rizzo likes to hike and Mrs. Rizzo likes to read science fiction. He likes to take his class on field trips and Mrs. Rizzo prefers to do experiments with her class.

Sometimes you will be asked how people or things are the same as well as how they are different. You can use another kind of graphic organizer to show this. It is called a Venn diagram.

The **Venn diagram** below shows how Mr. and Mrs. Rizzo are similar as well as how they are different.

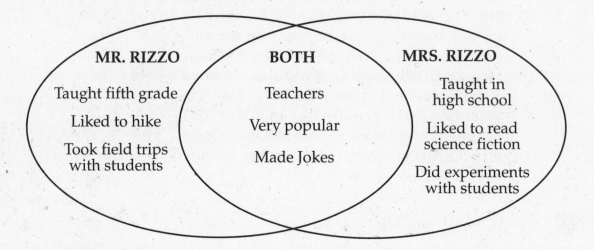

MR. RIZZO

Taught fifth grade

Liked to hike

Took field trips with students

BOTH

Teachers

Very popular

Made Jokes

MRS. RIZZO

Taught in high school

Liked to read science fiction

Did experiments with students

Notice that the diagram has two circles with a place in the middle where they overlap.

◆ In the parts of the circles that don't overlap, you list the differences between Mr. and Mrs. Rizzo.

◆ In the overlapping part, you list the things they have in common.

Now try the next example. Read the passage and complete the Venn diagram. Read this passage about Dr. Mendelsohn and his wife. Then study the Venn diagram that shows how the two people differed and how they were similar. Complete the diagram by finding something the two people had in common.

Example 2

Professor Mendelsohn and his wife are both interested in animals. Last Wednesday, they went to the museum early. The first exhibit they visited showed how whales live. Dr. and Mrs. Mendelsohn watched a film showing whales jumping high in the air. Then they went to hear the guide talk about dinosaurs.

The sign at the dinosaur exhibit said *"Tyrannosaurus rex, King of the Dinosaur World."* The guide described how this giant reptile got its meals and how it hunted and killed its prey. Dr. Mendelsohn looked at its long, sharp teeth and claws and its deadly tail. He knew he shouldn't be scared. A famous professor isn't supposed to be afraid of a museum exhibit, but he couldn't help it. Then he looked at his tiny wife. She walked up to the exhibit and looked closely at the claws. She studied how they looked with interest and enjoyment. Dr. Mendelsohn felt embarrassed.

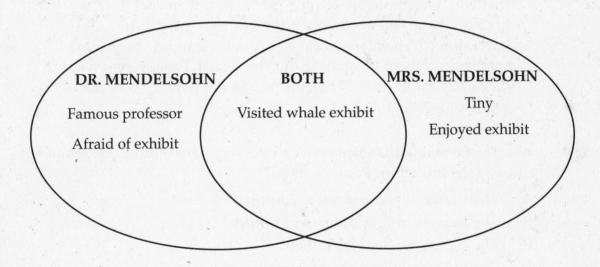

DR. MENDELSOHN

Famous professor

Afraid of exhibit

BOTH

Visited whale exhibit

MRS. MENDELSOHN

Tiny

Enjoyed exhibit

2 Find another detail that shows how Dr. Mendelsohn and his wife were similar.

    A.   embarrassed

    B.   thought whales were more interesting than dinosaurs

    C.   wanted to leave museum

    D.   interested in animal life

Choice D is correct. Both Dr. Mendelsohn and his wife like to study how animals live and survive.

The next question asks you to compare the ways in which potatoes are prepared.

Example 3

The potatoes grown by the early Indians in Peru looked more like sweet potatoes than our white potatoes. And they cooked them in a way unfamiliar to most of us. We like to eat our potatoes fried or mashed or boiled, or even baked in the oven. But the Indians in Peru prepared their potatoes in a way that you have probably never tried. Rather than cooking their potatoes fresh, they converted them into a dried form. After harvesting, the potatoes were spread on the ground, and people stamped on them to squeeze out the water. This process was repeated for five days. When the potato was ready, it was eaten like bread.

3 What is the main difference between the way we eat our potatoes and the way the Indians in Peru ate them?

    A.   The Indians in Peru dried their potatoes.

    B.   The Indians in Peru ate them mashed.

    C.   The Indians in Peru fried them.

    D.   The Indians in Peru ate them fresh.

 Your teacher will discuss your answer.

Later in **The Coach**, you will learn more about making comparisons and contrasts between people, places, times, and events.

HELPFUL HINTS
FOR DECIDING HOW THINGS ARE ALIKE
AND HOW THEY ARE DIFFERENT

---

1. See if a *chart* or a *Venn diagram* can help you to decide how things are alike and how they differ.

2. Check back in the selection for details if you can't remember why things are similar or different.

Selections for Practice

Selection 1

Andre is a star soccer player. His younger brother George likes to play soccer, too, but he's just a beginner. Sometimes they play on the same team and then Andre likes to show George how good he is. Andre moves very fast. He controls the ball with his foot, head and shoulders. He kicks goals with both his left foot and right foot. George loves to see Andre play.

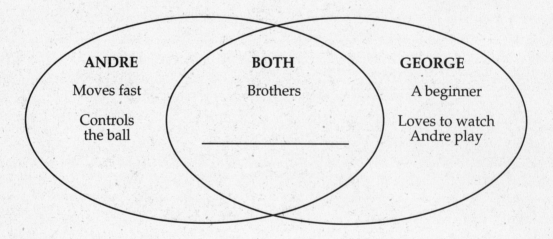

ANDRE

Moves fast

Controls the ball

BOTH

Brothers

_____

GEORGE

A beginner

Loves to watch Andre play

1 Which detail belongs in the empty space?

A. can't kick well

B. play on separate teams

C. play soccer

D. like to watch each other

Selection 2

I am just as happy as my brother Jamal. I get along with my parents just as well as he does and I have almost as many friends. Yet Jamal gets all the breaks and he doesn't even know how lucky he is.

First of all he's bigger and stronger and faster than most kids. Even when we were still in first grade, everyone always wanted Jamal on their team before they picked me. Also he's just better looking. And school comes very easy to him. I had a hard time learning to read, had to go to special classes, and my mother worked with me every night all through first and second grade. Jamal just naturally read everything without any trouble, and he never had problems in any other subjects either, except music.

Jamal doesn't like any music. He says it's all boring, but I think he really can't tell the difference between "The Star Spangled Banner" and "Row, Row, Row Your Boat." But I don't want to sound jealous. Jamal is not only my twin brother, he's also my best friend. I'm lucky to have a brother like Jamal.

2A READ THINK EXPLAIN How are Jamal and the speaker ALIKE?

_____

_____

_____

_____

_____

_____

2B READ THINK EXPLAIN   How do Jamal and the speaker DIFFER?

_____

_____

_____

_____

_____

_____

Part III: Literature

8 Understanding Story Plots

The **plot** tells what happens in a story. A plot may be simple, or it may be complex.

Here is a very simple plot:

> Peter loved to play the piano. He started playing when he was four.

No one would want to read this story. The plot isn't interesting enough.

Problems and Resolutions

Readers want a more complex and interesting story. They expect a plot with a **central problem** or conflict. In a good plot, things happen that create a central problem. The way the problem is worked out is called the **resolution** of the problem.

Read the next example. Notice how each event helps to develop the plot. Decide why Connie ran off the stage. What was the problem? How was it resolved?

Example 1

Connie was a young singer. Her first job was in Orlando. She got up to sing and saw dozens of people staring at her. She opened her mouth but nothing came out. Her body was shaking. She couldn't sing. She ran off the stage crying.

Connie decided to write songs instead of singing. She wrote 11 songs. Three of them were big hits. She likes writing songs. She is never scared and the songs are great.

1A What is the central problem in this story?

 A. Connie got nervous in front of an audience.

 B. Connie had three big hits.

 C. Connie was a young singer.

 D. Connie worked in Orlando.

The correct choice is A. The central problem is that when Connie got up to sing, nothing came out. Connie's problem was that she got nervous.

1B   How is the problem resolved?

    A.   She ran off the stage.

    B.   She decided to write songs.

    C.   Her body shook.

    D.   She sang in Orlando.

Choice B is the correct answer. Connie couldn't sing in front of audiences, but she could write songs. The problem in this selection is resolved when Connie changes what she wants to do.

Suppose you have to give a written answer to an **FCAT** question about a story's plot. Read the next example and answer the question.

Example 2

Paolo wasn't doing well in school. His grades had dropped a lot, just in the past four months. The teacher spoke to Paolo about what was wrong. Paolo said math was too hard and too boring. His teacher found out whenever Paolo looked at the blackboard and tried to understand a math problem, he couldn't see the numbers very well. And his head ached. Paolo sat in the back of the room.

His teacher put him in the front row. That helped a lot. The teacher also called his parents and told them they should take Paolo to the eye doctor. A week later, Paolo came in with his new glasses. After that it didn't matter where he sat. He could see everything well and he wasn't bored.

2 At the end of the story Paolo had new glasses. What problem did this solve? Use details and information from the story in your answer.

_____

_____

_____

_____

_____

_____

 Your teacher will discuss your answer.

HELPFUL HINTS
FOR UNDERSTANDING STORY PLOTS

---

1. Try to figure out the *central problem* or conflict in a passage. See if you can find the event that caused this problem.

2. Notice how a story ends. Many stories end by resolving their central problems.

Selections for Practice

Selection 1

Alex used to get in trouble often. He was absent a lot. But then he became a student in Mr. Moreno's class. Now Alex is completely different.

The only thing Alex liked was music. Mr. Moreno encouraged him to play the drums. He even helped Alex buy his own drum set. Also, Mr. Moreno didn't tell Alex what he was doing wrong all the time like the other teachers did. He helped Alex with his music. Then he left him alone to do his own thing.

Now Alex is into music all the time. He's too busy to get into trouble. Sometimes you can see him in the lunchroom. Everyone else is talking, but Alex is just humming and moving his fingers.

Alex is going to tour this summer with The Bosses. They say he's the one that makes the band hang together. And a lot of record companies have been interested in The Bosses since Alex joined. He's got the drive and energy everyone likes.

1A What was Alex's problem in this story?

    A. He was going to tour with The Bosses.

    B. He was in trouble all the time.

    C. He loved music.

    D. He hummed all the time.

1B How was Alex's problem resolved?

  A. He didn't come to school any more.
  B. He had a lot of energy.
  C. Mr. Moreno told him what he was doing wrong.
  D. Mr. Moreno worked with him on his music.

Selection 2

Tinnell saw the mountain bike in the window. It was great. It was just what he wanted. He came by every afternoon to look at it. The only problem was that it was expensive and he didn't have enough money saved to pay for it. His bike was getting old and needed a lot of work. A new bike would mean Tinnell could take part in the 8-mile race his school was holding. He thought he could win the race.

Tinnell finally decided to go inside the shop instead of just looking at the bike from outside the way he had done for the past two weeks. He said hello to Mr. Lucille, the owner.

"Boy, that's a beauty," Tinnell told Mr. Lucille. "I'd buy it in a minute if I had the money, but I'm short," said Tinnell. "Well now, how much can you afford?" the store owner asked. Tinnell told him exactly how much he had saved. Mr. Lucille thought a while and then asked, "Would you be willing to do some work for it?"

"Sure," said Tinnell. "Could you help me out on Saturdays?" Mr Lucille asked.

"Of course I could."

"Well," said Mr. Lucille, "Why don't you give me what you have and take the bike, and then work the rest off?"

"Do you mean it?" Tinnell asked, his eyes opening wide.

"Sure do," said Mr. Lucille.

2A   Tinnell's problem was that

    A.   he didn't have enough money for the bike.

    B.   he spent too much time looking at the bike.

    C.   he thought he could win the race.

    D.   he would have to work on Saturdays.

2B   How was Tinnell's problem resolved?

    A.   Tinnell saw a great new bike.

    B.   Tinnell wanted to be in the race.

    C.   Tinnell went inside the shop.

    D.   Mr. Lucille made a deal with Tinnell.

Selection 3

We were driving upstate to visit our cousins. Mom and Aunt Hilarie were in the back and Sid was at the wheel. We had gotten a late start. It was Friday afternoon and the middle of rush hour. At first it didn't seem so bad, but then the traffic began to get worse. Finally everything just stopped. It was like being stuck in a cup of molasses with no chance of escape. We sat in the car wishing we were already at the lake. Some of the motorists got out of their cars and started to talk to each other. It was a real mess.

Suddenly Aunt Hilarie remembered that there was a service road up ahead. If we could just get moving, we would be able to pull off the road and get out of the traffic. The cars started up very slowly and we inched forward until the turn off. No one else seemed to know about the road. Soon we were out of the traffic jam and on our way to a weekend of fun, swimming and fishing. We all felt a lot better then.

3A Why does the writer say, "It was a real mess"?

    A. She was stuck in a traffic jam.

    B. She wanted to stay at home.

    C. She wanted to drive the car.

    D. She wanted to get out of the car.

3B At the beginning of the story, the writer was concerned about the traffic. By the end of the story, she feels a lot better. What happened to change her mind? Use details and information from the story in your answer.

_____

_____

_____

_____

_____

_____

9 Comparing Characters, Settings, and Texts

Characters

In order to understand a story, you must understand the people in it. People give a story its meaning. The people in the story are called **characters.** Read Example 1 and decide who is the most important character in the story.

Example 1

Natalie loves animals. She likes to read about them and see movies about them. Sometimes Natalie goes to the movies with Fred. Fred loves all movies, but Natalie prefers movies about animals. Natalie loved the movie about a dog who was lost but found his way home. The dog in the movie reminded her of her dog, Ginger. But Ginger has never been lost. Natalie also has two cats, a rabbit she calls Polka Dot, and three fish. When she grows up she knows just what she wants to be—an animal doctor. She has always known what she wanted to do and even her mother believes she will do it.

 1A Who is the most important character in the story?

  A. Fred
  B. Ginger
  C. Natalie
  D. Polka Dot

C is the correct choice. All of the choices are mentioned in the story, but Natalie is the most important character because the author tells us most about her.

1B   Natalie is

    A.   sure of herself.

    B.   unfriendly.

    C.   lazy.

    D.   unable to make up her mind.

The correct choice is A. The selection says that Natalie knew what she wanted to be, that she has always known, and that her mother believes she will be an animal doctor. The other choices are incorrect.

You usually learn a lot about the important characters in a story. Authors describe them carefully.

Sometimes an author uses adjectives like "funny" or "slow" to describe people. At other times, the author describes how characters act without using words like "bored" or "happy." You can still figure out what these people are like from how they act.

Example 2

Pete couldn't believe he had missed the last shot. He was the reason his team lost. He couldn't stand to talk about it. When his teammates came up to him, he just stood there. He went home and didn't want to have dinner. He stayed in his room and looked through an old book. He didn't want to go to school the next day, but he finally decided he had to and got on the bus.

2   From this passage, you can guess that Pete is

    A.   easily amused.

    B.   tired.

    C.   sure of himself.

    D.   sad.

 Your teacher will discuss your answer.

Comparing Characters

When the **FCAT** asks you questions about people in a story, it will often ask you to compare one person to another. Try to see in what ways the characters are alike and in what ways they are different. How the characters differ from each other may be an important part of the story.

Read the next example, and then answer the question.

Example 3

Liela and Jiang were new students in Mrs. Goldstein's fourth-grade class. Liela had come to America from Egypt with her family. Jiang was from China. Both girls needed to practice their new language—English. Jiang could read English very well. She just felt embarrassed about speaking English out loud. She never raised her hand in class, even though she could answer most of the questions. Liela had a different attitude. She decided to speak English whenever she could. She answered questions in class, even if she had to ask the teacher to help her say what she meant. She also talked to the other kids in the class a lot.

3 How would you compare Liela and Jiang?
- A. Liela reads English better than Jiang.
- B. Jiang does not need to practice speaking English.
- C. Liela speaks English much more often than Jiang.
- D. Jiang does not like school.

 Your teacher will discuss your answer.

Comparing Settings

There are very few stories in which everything happens in the same place. More often, the action changes from one place to another. People travel from home to work; they visit their friends' homes; they go to movie theaters and sports arenas; they go to school and to church. The contrast between different **settings** may play an important role in a story.

Example 4

> The living room was downstairs. The heavy curtains over the windows shut out almost all the light. The heavy dark rugs made the room seem even more dark and sad to Elaine. She started upstairs and was surprised by how cheerful it was. Inside the tiny bedroom, the sun shone on the wooden floors and the brightly colored pillows decorated a spotlessly white reading chair.

  READ THINK EXPLAIN How does the upstairs bedroom differ from the downstairs living room? Use details and information from the story in your answer.

_____

_____

_____

_____

_____

 Your teacher will discuss your answer.

Comparing Events in Texts

The **FCAT** may ask you to compare the **events** that occur in two texts. When comparing texts, think about what the articles or stories have in common. Compare the characters and the settings.

Compare the events that occur and the themes of the passages.

Example 5

HECTOR'S SUCCESS

Hector is unusually quiet. Some people called him a nerd because he likes to study, doesn't like basketball or football, and doesn't like parties. So when we had School Talent Day, we thought Hector would sign up for the library. But instead he signed up to do comedy.

Hector was great. He's one of the funniest people I ever heard. He did imitations of all the teachers. They laughed so hard we thought the show would have to stop. Then he did an imitation of a man opening an umbrella in a hard rain with fierce winds.

He turned round and round on the stage with the umbrella opening and closing. It looked like he was being driven all across the stage. There wasn't a sound from the audience until Hector stopped moving, opened the umbrella, raised it above his head, breathed deeply, and smiled. Then everyone applauded.

After his success in the show, we thought Hector might act more lively in school and in class, but he's just as quiet as ever.

A BORN ARTIST

Eddie loved to draw. Every Saturday morning he took an art class given at the neighborhood center. But sometimes, Eddie overslept and got to class late. Last Saturday, Eddie was late, and the week before that he missed art altogether. Today he didn't oversleep, but he was still late. When he got to class, he hurried into the room and sat down hoping no one would notice, but the teacher turned to him and asked if he had done a drawing for the contest. Eddie said yes. "That's why I was late. I was working on it," he said. Then he pulled a beautiful drawing of a horse out of his bag.

5 READ THINK EXPLAIN   How are the two characters alike in these stories? Compare and contrast the events that occur to them. How are they similar? Use details and information from the stories in your answer.

_____

_____

_____

_____

_____

_____

 Your teacher will discuss your answer.

HELPFUL HINTS
FOR COMPARING CHARACTERS,
SETTINGS, AND TEXTS

1. A *character* is a person in a story or a poem. Look for parts of the story that tell you how the character acts.

2. When you read a story with two or more characters, decide how they are similar and how they are different.

3. When you have to compare *settings*, look out for clues that tell you where events take place and also when they take place. For example:

   ◆ Are there clues to tell you if a story takes place today or in the past?

   ◆ Are there words like light or dark, or hot or cold, to suggest the time of day or the time of year?

4. To compare *events* in texts, find ways the events are alike or different. Compare characters, settings, and themes.

Selections for Practice

Selection 1

Eva left Miami and moved to a new home in a small town in the Panhandle. The little town seemed unfamiliar and strange. The surrounding pine forest seemed not only alien, but also frightening. In fact, Eva was afraid of the forest. She had never feared city life, although she traveled in buses every day, surrounded by hundreds of unknown men and women.

Her new friend, Linda, was a life-long resident of this peaceful area. Linda had once taken a job in central Miami, but she soon found city life unbearably frantic and dangerous. Linda is a bird watcher, who spends many hours each week walking along trails looking for new birds. So far Linda hasn't been able to interest Eva in the joys of hiking and observing nature.

1 Eva differs from Linda because Eva

    A. dislikes buses.

    B. likes to hike.

    C. feels more secure in the city.

    D. is learning about birds.

Selection 2

Tinkerbell loved to be outdoors. She would bark until her master took her for a walk in the woods. She would romp up the hill and jump in the lake. She loved to leap over the dead trees lying in the forest. She was black and white and silky to the touch.

Lucky, on the other hand, was a little black dog who didn't like getting wet. Every time it rained, he would sit by the window and look out. When Tinkerbell went outside for her walk, Lucky would just sit and watch. He loved to eat, while Tinkerbell was fussy. Still they were friends and companions, and when Tinkerbell died, Lucky was sad.

2 | READ THINK EXPLAIN | How did Lucky differ from Tinkerbell?

_____

_____

_____

_____

_____

Selection 3

Read the next two letters and answer the questions.

A Letter from Lauderdale-by-the-Sea

Well, I'm settled in now and I love being here. The beach and ocean are great. I go walking every day along the shore and I jog around town. There was a great flea market here when I arrived and I bought two necklaces.

Tomorrow I am going snorkling. The boat takes you out to a reef and gives you the gear. The fish are supposed to be beautiful, and some people even see lobsters. They include lunch on board so it will probably be a great trip.

Aunt Julie lives right nearby and I spend a lot of time at her place. She's a great cook and makes me dinner almost every night. I help out by doing some gardening for her. I'm so glad I made the decision to live down here. It's very different than when you come just to visit, as I always have before. Now I feel I belong.

I have a good lead for a job. My interview is next week. Keep your fingers crossed.

It's been quite warm, and I have to be careful about the sun. But this beats the snow anyday.

Everyone is very friendly. I'll write more later.

Love,
Penny

My First Visit to Puerto Rico

Dear Tricia,

This is my first visit to Puerto Rico. It's been a trip worth waiting for. We arrived in San Juan early Sunday, but we spent little time there. We left early the next morning for the rain forests of El Yunque, the strangest place I've ever seen.

The forest was thickly covered with trees and shrubs. It rained heavily during the two hours we spent there, even though it was sunny everywhere else on the island.

We arrived in the city of Ponce on Monday night. That was the best part of the trip. I liked it most because I had heard so much about it when I was growing up. I could recognize some places just from what I had been told about them. I saw the house my father grew up in and visited the school he went to.

You know how bad my Spanish is, but I talked to Mrs. Ramirez, who used to teach my dad. I think she said he wasn't much of a student, but I'm not sure if I got it right.

On Wednesday, we went to Aguadilla, where my grandmother still lives. I loved walking its streets while my grandmother told me stories about her life.

Finally, we drove to Arecibo for some fishing and relaxation. Then back to San Juan to fly home.

Love,
Donna

3A READ THINK EXPLAIN Compare and contrast the settings described in these two letters. Are they alike? How are they different? Use details and information from the letters in your answer.

_____

_____

_____

_____

_____

3B READ THINK EXPLAIN Compare Penny's and Donna's experiences. How are they alike? How are they different? Use details and information from their letters in your answer.

_____

_____

_____

_____

_____

_____

_____

_____

_____

_____

10 Working Out Why Things Happen and What Their Effect Is

As you read, you often ask yourself why something happened. Authors will often hint at the reason why something is happening, and sometimes they even tell you clearly. If you find the word *because*, it may lead you to the answer.

Read the next passage and decide why Daisy Ashford is different from other writers.

Example 1

Daisy Ashford wrote a very popular book. It was called *The Young Visiters*. (Yes, that is how she spelled "Visitors.") It was a very funny book which sold more than 200,000 copies. Everyone said Daisy was a great writer.

Daisy Ashford was different from all other fine writers because she was only nine years old when she wrote the book. And she never wrote another book after that.

1 Daisy Ashford was different from other fine writers because

A. she wasn't very popular.

B. *The Young Visiters* sold more than 200,000 copies.

C. she was a child when she wrote her book.

D. her book was funny.

The correct choice is C. The passage says the reason Daisy Ashford was different form other fine writers was that she was only nine-years-old when she wrote her book.

There are many other key words and phrases used to indicate the *cause* or *effect* of an event. Some of these words and phrases are—

- ◆ Since
- ◆ As a result of
- ◆ The main reason is
- ◆ An important factor is

Sometimes you are asked why something happened and you don't find any key words like the ones above. When this happens, you must read carefully and work out the answer for yourself.

Read the next passage and decide why George Washington, our first President, found it hard to enjoy a meal.

Example 2

George Washington had false teeth. But he could never get his false teeth to work right. He tried using teeth taken from an elk, a kind of large deer. He tried wooden teeth. Everything he tried worked poorly and hurt his mouth. It was hard for him to ever enjoy a meal.

2 Why was it hard for George Washington to enjoy a meal? What did he do to try to correct this? Give details and information from the article.

_____

_____

_____

_____

_____

_____

 Your teacher will discuss your answer.

HELPFUL HINTS
FOR WORKING OUT WHY THINGS HAPPEN
AND WHAT THEIR EFFECT IS

1. Watch out for key words that show *cause* and *effect*. The words that follow the key word explain what caused something or what its effect was.

2. When there are no key words, ask yourself why an event occurred—its *cause*—or what was the result of an event—its *effect*. The answer will be there in the passage.

Selections for Practice

Selection 1

Lilly loves parrots. She likes to go to the pet store and look at them. She thinks that they are the most colorful things she has ever seen. One parrot says "Hi," to her. Another tries to peck at her hand. She asked her parents if she could have one, but they said no because parrots are so expensive. The pet store owner is nice. He lets Lilly play with the birds whenever she wants.

1 Why does Lilly love parrots?

A. They are colorful.

B. They are for sale in the pet store.

C. They peck at her.

D. The pet store owner is nice.

Selection 2

When I come home from school, I like to relax. I like to watch TV and then I like to go outside and play. But when I get home and my younger sister Charlotte is there, it's different. She always wants to play with me and she wants me to do everything she says.

I get tired of playing hopscotch and I hate playing dolls. I tell mom that I have to have some time to myself. But she just laughs and says not to worry about it.

2 READ THINK EXPLAIN Why can't the writer relax when she gets home from school? Give details and information from the article.

_____

_____

_____

_____

_____

_____

Selection 3

About 75 million people died of the Bubonic Plague during the 14th century. It was called the "Black Death." Half the population of Italy fell victim to the horrible disease. Most of them were buried without prayers. Dozens of victims would be put in one large grave. The plague caused high fevers, swollen glands, and dark splotches on the face. Most victims died within five days after getting the disease. The plague was spread by fleas from rats. Lack of cleanliness and rats accounted for the recurring epidemics throughout the 14th century.

3
Why do you think so many plague victims were buried without prayers? Give details and information from the article in your answer.

_____

_____

_____

_____

_____

11 Understanding Poetry and Poetic Language

What is Poetry?

Ordinary language is used mainly to pass along information. Poems, too, may provide information. But this is not their main purpose. **Poems** are about experience. Poets want us to share their experiences. These experiences might come from looking at nature or people, or from thinking about the past, or from dreaming.

Suppose we are interested in fruit trees. If all we want is information, we could turn to an encyclopedia or a gardening book. We might learn the names of different kinds of fruit trees. We could figure out when they flower and bear fruit. We might learn how tall they grow and what diseases attack them.

But if we want to grasp the experience of seeing a fruit tree, especially a fruit tree in blossom, we must turn to poetry.

These two lines about a cherry tree express the poet's experience of seeing a tree in blossom:

> Loveliest of trees, the cherry now
> Is hung with bloom along the bough,
> —From *A Shropshire Lad*, by A. E. Housman

Or if you want to sense the experience of winter, read these lines by William Shakespeare:

> When all aloud the wind doth blow,
> And coughing drowns the parson's saw*,
> And birds sit brooding in the snow,
> And Marian's nose looks red and raw,

*[the preacher's speech]

These two poets provide a good contrast between the sense of fruit trees in the spring and the bitter cold of a winter's day.

The next question asks you to distinguish between ordinary language and poetry.

Example 1

 Which of the following would you guess is a line of poetry?

    A.   At the end of the meal, the guests left the table.

    B.   The trees in the garden rained flowers.

    C.   The winner must receive all the votes.

    D.   The eagle can carry small animals with its talons.

The correct choice is B. The poet, Stephen Crane, manages to suggest the experience of being under a tree as the blossom falls from it. The other choices simply provide information.

So far we have talked about what a poem says. Poets also have special ways of arranging words when they write poetry.

Figurative Language

Writers, and especially poets, sometimes use words in an unusual fashion where the words don't mean exactly what they say. We call this special use of words poetic or **figurative language**.

For example, you might read:

Betty ran through the house like a hurricane.

The word hurricane isn't used to mean a real hurricane. Betty may be in a hurry, but she could never have the force of a hurricane.

But you understand what the writer means—Betty was in a hurry.

Using Imagery to Make Comparisons

When a writer compares one thing to another, and uses the words "like" or "as," he is using a writing technique called a **simile**.

Read Example 2 and notice how the author describes the wind.

Example 2

> Suddenly the wind died down—like a frantic stallion that had worn itself out and could no longer rear up and kick. It was a welcome change to the crew. They hoped the wind was tamed and that the rest of the trip to the islands would be a fair run.

The writer compares the wind to a horse. Instead of saying that the wind was strong or that it was blowing hard, the writer uses figurative language to get our attention.

Read the passage again and then answer the question.

2 When you read that the wind was "like a frantic stallion that had worn itself out," you can guess that the wind

  A. had died down.

  B. was very strong.

  C. was threatening to blow hard.

  D. was beginning to get worse.

Choice A is correct. The wind was like a frantic stallion that had worn itself out. This means the wind was no longer blowing hard and had died down. This is the meaning of the simile that the poet uses.

Sometimes figurative language can make a poem hard to understand. It needs to be read and read again. The lines from the next poem describe a train journey in the old West. Read it as many times as you need to and decide what it means.

Example 3

EL PONIENTE
by Ruth Comfort Mitchell

1. Beneath the train the miles are folded by;
2. High and still higher through the vibrant air
3. We mount and climb. Silence and brazen glare;
4. Desert and sagebrush; cactus, alkali,
5. Tiny, low-growing flowers brilliant, dry;
6. A vanishing coyote, lean and spare,
7. Lopes slowly homeward with a backward stare,
8. To jigsaw hills cut sharp against the sky,
9. In the hard turquoise rides a copper sun.

3A The poet describes the land through which the train is passing as

    A. totally empty.

    B. cold and dreary.

    C. filled with rivers and lakes.

    D. a silent desert.

The train is passing through the desert; the poet describes its silence. Choice D is correct. The land is not empty—the traveler sees plants and a coyote—so Choice A is not correct. Nothing in the poem suggests that it is cold and there is no mention of water, so the other two choices are also incorrect.

3B What is the "hard turqoise" in line 9?

    A. a precious jewel

    B. the sea

    C. the sky

    D. the endless desert

The full line reads, "In the hard turquoise rides a copper sun." Your own experience tells you that the sun is in the sky. Also, you learn in the previous line that the poet is looking at the hills and the sky. You may also know that turquoise is a blue stone, but the other clues lead you to the right answer, even if you don't. Choice C is correct.

You read about the "jigsaw hills cut sharp against the sky" where the coyote lives. Why does the poet describe the hills in this way?

    A.   to suggest that they look like the zig-zag teeth of a jigsaw

    B.   to stress that they are very far away

    C.   to show that they are smooth and soft

    D.   to show that they puzzle her

Choice A is correct. The teeth of a jigsaw (a type of saw) are shaped like the letter V.

This is an example of another technique used by writers called a **metaphor**.

When you say that one thing is like another without using the words "like" or "as," you are using a metaphor.

Similes and metaphors are not the only literary techniques writers use. Others include: **symbolism**, where a writer uses one thing to represent another; **personification**, where the writer describes objects using human feelings and characteristics; and **alliteration**, where the writer uses certain words and sounds together, many of the words beginning with the same letter.

HELPFUL HINTS
FOR UNDERSTANDING POETRY
AND POETIC LANGUAGE

---

1. The term *figurative language* means using words and phrases in an unusual way where they don't mean exactly what they say.

2. Authors use figurative language to make their writing more colorful, powerful, and interesting. Some literary techniques writers use are *simile, metaphor, symbolism, personification,* and *alliteration*.

3. You can usually use context clues to understand this language.

4. Often, you need to read the whole passage or poem to understand words that are used figuratively.

Selections for Practice

Selection 1

The Paiute Indian people lived in the desert, near the mountains. In the summer, sheep and deer lived on the mountain grass. The Paiute people ate well. But in the winter, the sheep and deer moved to the south. The mountain was covered with snow, and there was little to eat. The Paiute wanted warm weather to return so they could leave their huts and walk again on the grass.

THE GRASS ON THE MOUNTAIN

1   Oh, long, long
2   The snow has covered the mountains.
3   The deer have come down
4   And the bighorn sheep.
5   They have followed the sun to
6   the south.

7   Oh, long, long
8   We have eaten old seeds
9   And dried deer's flesh that
10   we killed last summer.

11   We are tired of our huts
12   And the smoky smell of our clothes.
13   We are sick with desire for the sun.
14   We long for grass to grow
15   again on the mountain.

 1A Who is speaking in this poem?

     A. a farmer who is planting seeds

     B. a hunter who is camping out in the woods

     C. a Paiute who is tired of winter

     D. a Paiute who enjoys cooking

1B What does the poet mean when he says, "We are sick with desire for the sun..." in line 13?

A. The poet doesn't feel very well.

B. The poet wants to get a tan.

C. The poet wants nice weather.

D. The poet is worried it is too hot.

Selection 2

Mara's headache was worse. It was a pounding nightmare that she couldn't escape. Nothing helped. She swallowed pills, took walks in the fresh air, drank tea, and took herbal cures. She couldn't think clearly. Why was this happening to her?

2 READ THINK EXPLAIN Why would you guess the writer describes a headache as a "pounding nightmare"?

_____

_____

_____

_____

_____

Selection 3

I WANDERED LONELY AS A CLOUD
by William Wordsworth

1   I wandered lonely as a cloud
2   That floats on high o'er vales and hills.
3   When all at once I saw a crowd,
4   A host of golden daffodils;
5   Beside the lake, beneath the trees,
6   Fluttering and dancing in the breeze.

3A A cloud just moves around in the sky. It wanders to wherever the wind blows it. What does the poet mean when he says he "wandered lonely as a cloud"?

A.   He is walking by himself. He isn't walking to any place special.

B.   He feels confused. He is looking for his friends.

C.   He feels strong and very important.

D.   He feels angry. He wants people to pay attention to him.

3B What does the poet tell us in lines 4, 5, and 6?

A.   Why he felt so cold

B.   Why he likes to dance

C.   Where he saw the flowers

D.   When he liked to swim

Part IV: Practice Tests

HINTS FOR TAKING FCAT READING TESTS

◆ Relax. Everyone gets nervous about tests. It's natural. Try to relax and not worry.

◆ Listen carefully to the directions. Be sure to read all the directions you find in the test book. Ask your teacher to explain any directions you do not understand.

◆ Read each story and question very carefully. You may look back at the story as often as you like.

◆ Think about each question. If you cannot answer a question right away, give yourself some time to think about it.

◆ Plan your time. If you do not know the answer to a question, skip it and go back to it later. Answer the questions you are sure of first.

◆ Keep a positive state of mind. Some questions will be hard to answer and others will be easy. Just do your best.

◆ When you answer a multiple-choice question:

   • fill in the bubble of the answer you choose on your answer sheet.

   • make sure you have darkened the bubble completely.

   • do not leave any stray marks on the page.

◆ When you answer a "Read, Think, and Explain" question:

   • read the passage and the question carefully.

   • think about the information it contains.

   • organize your thoughts.

   • plan your answer.

   • write your answer in the lines provided in the answer sheet.

   • make sure you stay on target and answer the question that is asked

Answer sheets are provided following the tests.

Practice Test 1

Maya Angelou is one of the greatest poets of this country. In this poem, the poet talks about overcoming prejudice. Read the poem, then do Numbers 1 through 5.

FROM "STILL I RISE"
by Maya Angelou

You may write me down in history
With your bitter, twisted lies,
You may trod me in the very dirt
But still, like dust, I'll rise.

Does my sassiness upset you?
Why are you beset with gloom?
'Cause I walk like I've got oil wells
Pumping in my living room.

Just like moons and like suns,
With the certainty of tides,
Just like hopes springing high,
Still I'll rise.

1 The poet says she walks like she has "oil wells pumping in her living room." What does she mean by this?

A. She is shy.
B. She feels strong and powerful.
C. She doesn't have much fun.
D. She is full of fear.

2 Read this quote.

> **Just like moons and like suns,**
> **With the certainty of tides,**

Why do you think the poet compares herself to moons, suns, and tides?

F.   Moons, suns, and tides are dangerous.

G.   All are shown on TV and in the movies.

H.   They are all very beautiful.

I.   Moons, suns, and tides can be depended upon.

3 The title "Still I Rise" means

A.   the poet has the power to overcome difficulties.

B.   the poet will go to heaven.

C.   the poet is beautiful like the moon and the sun.

D.   the poet feels happy in the dust.

4 To whom is the poet talking when she says "You may write me down in history/With your bitter, twisted lies..."?

F.   to children in elementary school

G.   to people who are minorities

H.   to people who put down minorities

I.   to sick people

5  Why does the poet say she will rise? Why do you think this is important to her? Give details and information from the poem in your answer.

Read this article about the first successful airplane flight. Then answer Numbers 6 through 14.

THE WRIGHT BROTHERS

The first time an airplane flew in the air was in North Carolina. It happened on December 17, 1903 in Kitty Hawk. Two brothers named Wilbur and Orville Wright had invented this airplane. Others had tried before these two men.* But no other plane had ever stayed off the ground for long.

The airplane the Wright brothers made was small and light. It could only hold one person. Orville won a coin toss. He got to be the pilot. The plane flew 120 feet on its first flight. It stayed up in the air only 12 seconds. But later in the day, the plane did better. It made a flight of 852 feet in 59 seconds.

Wilbur and Orville were interested in machines from the time they were children. When they first decided they wanted to build an airplane, they read everything they could find on this topic. Then they built gliders. Gliders are planes without engines. They sail on the wind. The Wright brothers learned a lot about flying from gliders.

Then they decided to build a plane with an engine that burned gasoline. When their plane was the first one ever to fly, they were not surprised. They had studied hard and knew what they were doing.

It took awhile for people to realize how important the Wright's airplane was. Meanwhile, the brothers kept working

*Leonardo da Vinci, the great Italian artist and inventor, was among the earliest people to try to find a way to fly. He designed a kind of helicopter, a machine with wings that moved, and a glider. Unfortunately, none of them worked. Da Vinci wasn't the only one interested in flight. Before the Wright brothers' discovery, some inventors even lost their lives trying to get their planes to fly.

on their plane. Finally, in 1905, it flew for 38 minutes and traveled a little over 24 miles. Then the newspapers began to report on what they were doing. Before this, only scientists had realized the importance of the Wright brothers invention.

The Wright brothers kept working on their plane and making it better over the years. In 1909, they started their own company to make airplanes. It was very successful. The two brothers became famous. They are both considered the inventors of the airplane.

The airplane that Orville and Wilbur flew that day in 1903 is now in the National Air and Space Museum in Washington, D.C. You can see it if you visit our capital. In North Carolina, you can visit the sandy hill where the plane first flew. It is in the Wright Brothers Memorial in Kitty Hawk.

6 This selection is mostly about

    A.   what gliders are and why they are important

    B.   how airplanes stay up in the air

    C.   how the Wright brothers invented the airplane

    D.   how airplanes are made

7 Why did the Wright brothers study flying?

    F.   They wanted to build an airplane.

    G.   They had to study this for school.

    H.   They wanted to join the Air Force.

    I.   They were tired of selling bicycles.

8 Read these sentences from the article.

Then they built gliders. Gliders have no engines. They sail on the wind.

How are gliders different from airplanes?

    A.   Gliders have pilots.

    B.   Planes are larger.

    C.   Planes have engines.

    D.   Gliders are more expensive than airplanes.

9 Newspapers became interested in the Wright brothers' plane

    F.   after the Wright brothers became famous.

    G.   after the Wright brothers' plane flew for 12 seconds

    H.   after the Wright brothers' plane flew for 24 miles

    I.   before scientists were interested in the plane

10 You read that the Wright brothers were not surprised when their plane flew. What detail supports this idea?

    A.   They had studied flying very carefully.

    B.   They were always very sure of themselves.

    C.   They knew they would be lucky.

    D.   The weather was very good for flying.

11 The author seems to feel that

    F.   the Wright Brothers were smarter than everybody else.

    G.   the Wright Brothers worked hard.

    H.   the Wright Brothers were lucky.

    I.   the Wright Brothers had more money than other inventors.

12 READ THINK EXPLAIN Read the information in the footnote. Why do you think so many people wanted to fly? What kind of sacrifices did people make? Use details and information from the article and the footnote in your answer.

13 Which is an opinion?

    A.   The Wright brothers started their own company in 1909.

    B.   Gliders are planes without engines.

    C.   The Wright brothers' airplane was important.

    D.   In 1905, the Wright brothers' plane flew for 38 minutes.

14 If you wanted to learn more about this selection which resource reference would you use?

F.   a medical encyclopedia

G.   a general encyclopedia

H.   an atlas

I.   a dictionary

15 Why does it seem likely that the Wright Brothers were among the first people to succeed at flying?

You read one passage from Charlie and the Chocolate Factory earlier in this book. Here is another one. In this part of the book, the owner of the chocolate factory has promised that the five people who find the Golden Tickets in his candy bars will have a lifetime supply of candies. Read it and then do Numbers 16 through 22.

Charlie burst through the front door, shouting, "Mother! Mother! Mother!"

Mrs. Bucket was in the old grandparents' room, serving them their evening soup.

"Mother!" yelled Charlie, rushing in on them like a hurricane. "Look! I've got it! Look, Mother, Look! The last Golden Ticket! It's mine! I found some money in the street and I bought two candy bars and the second one had the Golden Ticket and there were crowds of people all around me wanting to see it and the shopkeeper rescued me and I ran all the way home and here I am! IT'S THE FIFTH GOLDEN TICKET, MOTHER, AND I'VE FOUND IT!"

Mrs. Bucket simply stood and stared, while the four old grandparents, who were sitting up in bed balancing bowls of soup on their laps, all dropped their spoons with a clatter and froze against their pillows

For about ten seconds there was absolute silence in the room. Nobody dared to speak or move. It was a magic moment.

Then, very softly, Grandpa Joe said, "You're pulling our legs, Charlie, aren't you? You're having a little joke?"

"I am not!" cried Charlie, rushing up to the bed and holding out the large and beautiful Golden Ticket for him to see.

Grandpa Joe leaned forward and took a close look, his nose almost touching the ticket. The others watched him, waiting for the verdict.

Then very slowly, with a slow and marvelous grin spreading all over his face, Grandpa Joe lifted his head and looked straight at Charlie. The color was rushing to his cheeks, and his eyes were wide open, shining with joy, and in the center of each eye, right in the very center, in the black pupil, a little spark of wild excitement was slowly dancing. Then the old man took a deep breath, and suddenly, with no warning whatsoever, an explosion seemed to take place inside him. He threw up his arms and yelled "Yippeeeeeeeeeeeeeeeeeeeeeeeeeeee!" And at the same time, his long bony body rose up out of the bed and his bowl of soup went flying into the face of Grandma Josephine, and in one fantastic leap, this old fellow of ninety-six and a half, who hadn't been out of bed these last twenty years, jumped on to the floor and started doing a dance of victory in his pajamas.

16 Why did Charlie rush through the door?

A. He was excited.

B. He was late.

C. He was hungry.

D. He was always hurrying.

17 At first Grandpa Joe said, "You're pulling our legs," to Charlie. Why did he say this?

F. He couldn't believe it was true.

G. He was in a lot of pain.

H. He wanted some candy.

I. Charlie liked to tell lies.

18 Where did the Golden Ticket come from?

  A. the crowd

  B. the street

  C. the first candy bar

  D. the second candy bar

19 Why did the grandparents drop their spoons?

  F. They fell asleep.

  G. They didn't like the soup.

  H. They were very old and feeble.

  I. They were surprised.

20 READ THINK EXPLAIN What did Grandpa Joe do when he heard the news that Charlie had found the Golden Ticket? Use details and information from the story in your answer.

21 Think about what is going on in this passage. Then read this sentence.

The others watched him, waiting for the verdict.

What is a verdict?

  A. a sadness

  B. something very old

  C. a decision

  D. a trip

22 What happened last?

  F. Charlie found the Golden Ticket.

  G. Grandpa Joe got out of bed.

  H. Grandpa Joe did a victory dance.

  I. Charlie raced home.

This selection tells about Andrew Jackson and how he became President of the United States in 1828. Read it and answer Numbers 23 through 31.

THE AGE OF JACKSON
by Hilarie Staton

A NEW KIND OF PRESIDENT EMERGES

Andrew Jackson was elected President of the United States in 1828. He was a new kind of President. Our first Presidents were wealthy landowners. They had big farms and they consorted with other gentlemen land owners. They didn't know many ordinary Americans. But Jackson was different. He was surrounded by people from all walks of life, not just wealthy farmers. For the first time in America, power was in the hands of the "common man," not the "gentleman." This was the time of the rise of the common man.

Right after the American Revolution, most of the people who lived in the 13 states could not vote. Only white men who owned property had such a privilege. By 1828 things were a little better. Women, African Americans, and Native Americans still could not vote. But now white men with little or no property could vote. The new voters were small farmers and factory workers, and they wanted new laws and new politicians. Jackson was their kind of leader.

THE PRESIDENTIAL ELECTION OF 1824

Jackson ran for President in 1824. He ran against three candidates: John Quincy Adams, who was the Harvard-educated son of a former President; William Crawford; and Henry Clay. Although Jackson got the most popular votes, he wasn't elected President. No one got more than half the electoral votes, so the House of Representatives had to pick a winner. Clay supported Adams, and his votes tipped the balance. Jackson felt he was cheated, but Adams was the new President.

THE PRESIDENTIAL ELECTION OF 1828

In 1828, Jackson ran again. This time he was determined to beat John Quincy Adams and to succeed him as the new American President. Jackson and his supporters formed a new political party. They called it the Democratic Party. The Democrats said they were the party of the common man. They wanted the support of the new voters.

Andrew Jackson worked hard to win. He spoke to factory workers and farmers who had never voted before. He spoke to newspaper reporters. He traveled around giving talks and speaking to people all over the country. He attended meetings everywhere, while his opponent stayed in the White House. President Adams didn't want to give talks or speak to ordinary Americans or attend meetings. As a consequence, Jackson won the election. He had changed the way candidates run for office. From his time on, all candidates would give talks and meet people. They would try to show voters they understood what America needed.

Jackson knew how to persuade voters, even though he never gave his opinions about the things on which many people disagreed, like slavery. Some people thought he was against it, even though he owned a plantation with slaves. And the lowly American worker was certain he supported their interests, although he himself had made a fortune and was a wealthy man.

JACKSON, THE HERO

People may not have known where Jackson stood on many of the issues. But that wasn't important. Jackson was a great military leader who had won a major victory in Louisiana. He had shown he was tough. Once he fought a duel with a lawyer

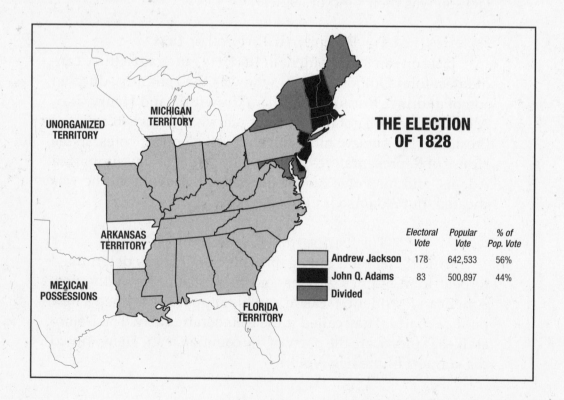

THE ELECTION OF 1828

	Electoral Vote	Popular Vote	% of Pop. Vote
Andrew Jackson	178	642,533	56%
John Q. Adams	83	500,897	44%
Divided			

who was a crack shot. The lawyer fired first and wounded Jackson badly. But Jackson stood up, waited until his head cleared, and killed his opponent. Some said he was too much a fighter to be a good President, but others admired him. They called him "Old Hickory" because hickory is a strong wood. He got votes, not because of his ideas, but because people respected and trusted him.

AFTER THE ELECTION

Before taking the job as President, it is customary to have a celebration. Although the inaugural parties before Jackson was elected were usually restricted to a few people, Jackson's inaugural was a big bash. Thousands of his fans came to Washington to welcome him to the presidency. Some came wearing muddy boots from their long trip. They were welcomed, but the White House rugs were destroyed. The large crowds broke furniture, knocked food and drink onto curtains and floors, and practically tore the White House into pieces.

After the election, Jackson became a tough President. He refused to go along with Congress. He felt he was defending the common man. He made many changes. People disagree about whether his changes were good or bad. But they all agree that with Jackson, a new era had begun.

23 Read this line.

For the first time in America, power was in the hands of the "common man," not the "gentleman."

Who were the "common men"?

A. College students and highly educated businessmen

B. Shopkeepers and small farmers

C. Slaves

D. Wealthy landowners

24 What is the main idea of the section called "The Presidential Election of 1828"?

   F. Andrew Jackson helped form the Democratic Party.

   G. Jackson won because he had the support of the "common man."

   H. Jackson campaigned by speaking to ordinary people.

   I. Ordinary people no longer wanted to vote.

25 Look at the map of the 1828 election.

   Which of the following statements is true?

   A. Jackson lost the election.

   B. Adams won most of the states.

   C. Most Southern states voted for Jackson.

   D. Illinois voted for Adams.

26 An era is

   F. a kind of climate.

   G. a period of time.

   H. a type of plant or animal.

   I. something very old.

27 Why was Jackson called "Old Hickory"? Use details and information from the article in your answer.

28 What is the main purpose of this selection?

   A. to explain the meaning of the words "common man"

   B. to tell how Andrew Jackson killed a lawyer in a duel

   C. to show how Andrew Jackson changed politics and the presidency

   D. to show why Jackson lost the election in 1824

29 What happened after Jackson became president?

    F.   He became less interested in the common people.

    G. He tried to get rid of slavery.

    H. He only invited the rich and powerful to his inauguration.

    I.   He made changes that he thought benefited the common man.

30 Immediately after the Revolutionary War ended, who could vote?

    A. every adult except slaves

    B. every adult except slaves and women

    C. every white adult male

    D. every white adult male who owned property

31 READ THINK EXPLAIN Why didn't Andrew Jackson discuss slavery in 1828?

    Give details and information from the article in your answer.

Here is a story about a wealthy man and a poor tailor. Read *Not Even For Gold*. Then do Numbers 32 through 40.

NOT EVEN FOR GOLD

A wealthy old man lived in a grand house next door to a poor tailor and his wife. The tailor sang to himself as he went about his work. From morning to night, the wealthy man heard his neighbor singing.

The tailor enjoyed singing. It seemed to make his work go faster, and it drove away all his cares. When he sang, the tailor did not worry about how much he had earned that week. He did not worry about how many bills he had left to pay. He did not think of anything except his singing and his work.

In the early afternoon, the wealthy old man would take a nap. But at the same time, the tailor would be working and singing. Whenever the tailor hit a high note, his neighbor woke up. The old man was very upset at being jolted out of his sleep. It made him feel terrible for the rest of the day. Day after day, the tailor woke up the wealthy old man, and the wealthy old man felt worse and worse.

At last, the old man could stand it no longer. He went to knock at the tailor's door. "My sleep is worth a great deal to me," the rich man told his neighbor. "I'll give you eight pieces of gold a day if you'll stop singing."

"What a great piece of luck!" the tailor thought. "Now I'll be able to pay my bills!"

The next day the tailor worked, but this time he did not sing. The wealthy old man slept as soundly as a baby. When he woke up, he felt better than he had in years.

"A good nap is well worth the price I'm paying," he thought with a smile.

But the tailor was not smiling. Now that he could not sing, he began to worry about all sorts of things. Also, the joy vanished from his work. His needle dragged as he worked. By the end of one day without singing, the tailor felt worse than he ever had in his life.

The tailor went to the wealthy man's house. "I know that you need your sleep," he said. "But I need my song to be happy. I must go on singing. But I have a plan. While you're napping, I'll just hum softly. That way, you'll have your sleep, and I'll have my song."

Then he handed the gold back to his neighbor. "I can't trade my song for anything in the world," the tailor said, "not even for gold!"

32 This *story* is mostly about

  F. a tailor who liked to sing

  G. a greedy man

  H. a rich person who didn't like tailors

  I. a clever tailor

33 READ THINK EXPLAIN   Why did the wealthy man offer the tailor gold?

34 Read this line.

"What a great piece of luck!" the tailor thought.

What did the tailor mean by a *piece of luck*?

  A. One of the gold pieces was lucky.

  B. He would be able to pay his bills.

  C. He thought his singing was worth the money.

  D. He wanted to be like the rich man.

35 Why did the wealthy man say that "a good nap is well worth the price I'm paying"?

  F. He thought that sleeping was better than sewing.

  G. He wanted the tailor to stop sewing.

  H. He was very generous.

  I. He finally had some rest.

36 When the tailor sang he

    A. bothered his wife.

    B. was off key.

    C. didn't sew very well.

    D. didn't worry.

37 The tailor gave the gold back to the wealthy man because

    F. he thought he was given too many gold pieces

    G. he wanted to sing while he worked

    H. he couldn't sew anymore

    I. he wanted to have the wealthy man's house

38 At the end, the tailor was shown as

    A. angry

    B. dishonest

    C. proud

    D. wise

39 If the wealthy man said he would give the tailor 20 gold coins if he would stop humming, what do you think the tailor would have done?

    F. tell the rich man he wanted more gold coins

    G. refuse the gold and continue to hum

    H. take the gold and put it in the bank

    I. give the gold to his wife so she could buy a new outfit

40   Why did the author call this story "Not Even For Gold"? Use details and information from the passage in your answer.

Read the next article about Charles Ringling. Then do Numbers 41 through 45.

I LOVE A CIRCUS!

The Ringling Brothers loved the world of the circus and its performers. And their name is well known among circus lovers. John, and his brother Charles, were two of the seven Ringling brothers who formed the Ringling Brothers Barnum & Bailey Circus. The circus was billed as "The Greatest Show On Earth" and was world famous. It traveled everywhere with its high wire performers, its lion tamers, its elephants, and its clowns. Most of the performances were done in the warm weather. In the winter, the circus traveled south. Both Charles and John liked to come to Sarasota, Florida, and they made it their headquarters for the winter, bringing many circus people and friends with them.

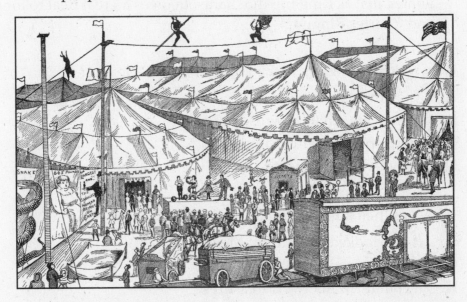

John and Charles liked the area so much they made great plans to turn the small fishing village of Sarasota into a place that people would come to visit. They owned a lot of land and they helped build many landmarks that still exist today.

One of John's projects was the building of the causeway or bridge connecting the mainland and Lido Key, a small island off the coast. Some people say that John used his circus elephants to help build the bridge. That must have been quite a sight!

John and his wife Mable built a beautiful mansion, called Ca'd'zan or "House of John," overlooking the Gulf of Mexico.

They filled it with art treasures, and famous people, including circus performers, came to stay with them as their guests. Everyone wanted to go to the Ringling's parties.

After Charles' death, John became director of the circus. When John got older, he decided to will his property to the state of Florida. After he and his wife died, it was made into a museum.

In 1948, the State of Florida honored John Ringling by establishing a circus collection. The circus museum, nearby the Ringling home, has many wonderful and rare items, like posters, photographs, circus wagons, and costumes and props used by famous performers.

Today, Sarasota is still a center for the circus. Besides the circus museum, there is a world-famous clown college. And many well-known circus performers make their home in Sarasota, like the Wallendas, Zacchinis, and Cristianis, in the winter, just as Ringling did. Sarasota owes a great deal to John and Charles Ringling.

41 Why was the Ringling name known by circus lovers?

A. They owned a circus.

B. They were circus clowns.

C. They opened a circus museum.

D. They lived in Sarasota.

42 Why was the mansion called Ca'd'zan or "House of John?"

F. It overlooked the Gulf of Mexico.

G. It was named for John Ringling.

H. It contained many art treasures.

I. It was very old and valuable.

43 Read this line.

> **John decided to will his property to the state of Florida.**

When someone wills something, they

- **A.** sell it at an auction.
- **B.** have it destroyed.
- **C.** leave it to someone after they die.
- **D.** make it bigger.

44 There were rumors about what John Ringling used to build the causeway. Which picture best illustrates the rumor about how the causeway was built?

F.

H.

G.

I.

45 The article says that "Sarasota owes a great deal to John and Charles Ringling." Why is this true? What did the Ringlings do to help Sarasota? Use details and information in your answer.

These letters were written by two people who immigrated to this country. Read them and do Numbers 46 through 50.

LIFE IN NEW YORK CITY
by Eddie Miranda

My family and I came to New York City from Puerto Rico. Here it is more exciting. You can meet more people. There are more places to go. There are many different things to do. That makes life more interesting and exciting. You can have a better life here. But I don't know if we'll stay.

Life here is different. The climate of Puerto Rico is better. It is much warmer there. You can spend more time outside and the winter wasn't so bad. Some of my friends went back because they want to live in a warmer place.

The culture of New York City is totally different. We live in a big building. We are always with people from different nationalities. We share our life with different people. We pick up customs from other countries. After a while, we are totally different people. I do not like this.

School is very hard. School is hard for all of us, not just the children. The language is different, the teachers are rushed, the whole approach is different. Because school is so hard, we have many problems.

Also, many people treat us badly. They act like we are foreigners. We have a right to live here and work here. People do not know this. They ask to see our green cards. They ask for work permits. We often get mad at how badly people treat us.

People act better in Puerto Rico. We lived in a small place in Puerto Rico. Everyone knew my parents. So we had to be quiet. We had to do things right. Here it is different. Nobody knows who you are. People say, "Do what you want. Who cares?" So people sometimes act crazy here. In Puerto Rico, we act better and I prefer this.

In spite of everything, many of us like it here. Most of us are happy to be in New York.

FINDING A LIFE IN THE NEW WORLD
by Theresa Avena

I was nine when I came to America. My father had left our native Italy first. He knew the New World would have many opportunities for us. He could find good work and one day he said we would have our own house. We missed him a lot. But it was the only way he could save enough money to send for us. I remember the voyage to New York City very well. The ship was crowded and we had to sleep altogether on the floor. But the idea of coming to America was wonderful to me. It was a dream come true.

I remember how I was standing on deck and looking out and there it was, the wonderful lady—the Statue of Liberty, shining in the sun. I cried with joy. My father met us and took us straight to the shop where he was the head barber. Everything smelled of soap and the men had their faces all lathered up.

My first day at school wasn't much fun. The kids all stared at me. I couldn't speak any English and no one spoke Italian. I didn't know how to tell the teacher I needed to use the bathroom. It was horrible. Getting to school was even worse than being there. My mother couldn't take me to school so I had to go myself and I kept getting lost. And people sent me to the wrong school. I remember it like it was just yesterday.

I couldn't eat the food. It was nothing I liked and I didn't like how it smelled. I wanted to go home very badly.

But eventually, like everyone else, my English got better, my friends made school fun, and I got to like the food.

I studied very hard when I wasn't helping my mother with cleaning and cooking. I got very good grades. I got a scholarship to college. Even there, kids thought I was funny. Most came from families who had lived in America a very long time. They made some jokes about me I didn't like. But they were impressed when I graduated with honors. Now I'm a teacher and I try to help students adjust to new situations. I can do things here I could never have done in the old country. America had been good to me.

46 Why does Eddie Miranda's family remain in the United States?

A. Work is harder to find.

B. They are happy.

C. They are treated very well.

D. They like the climate.

47 How was life different in New York City from Puerto Rico for Eddie Miranda?

F. The people were very friendly.

G. The buildings were smaller.

H. School was harder.

I. His family was richer.

48 Why did Theresa Avena's father come to America before his wife and children?

A. He liked to be alone.

B. There was no room on the ship.

C. He needed to find a job.

D. He needed to make money so that they could come too.

How are the settings in these letters different? In what ways are they the same? Use details and information from the letters in your answer.

  How are the events in Eddie Miranda's and Theresa Avena's lives similar? How are they different? Use details and information from the letters in your answer.

Practice Test 1 Answer Sheet

1 Ⓐ Ⓑ Ⓒ Ⓓ   **2** Ⓕ Ⓖ Ⓗ Ⓘ   **3** Ⓐ Ⓑ Ⓒ Ⓓ

4 Ⓕ Ⓖ Ⓗ Ⓘ

5 READ THINK EXPLAIN

6 Ⓐ Ⓑ Ⓒ Ⓓ   **7** Ⓕ Ⓖ Ⓗ Ⓘ   **8** Ⓐ Ⓑ Ⓒ Ⓓ

9 Ⓕ Ⓖ Ⓗ Ⓘ   **10** Ⓐ Ⓑ Ⓒ Ⓓ   **11** Ⓕ Ⓖ Ⓗ Ⓘ

12 READ THINK EXPLAIN

13 Ⓐ Ⓑ Ⓒ Ⓓ   **14** Ⓕ Ⓖ Ⓗ Ⓘ

15

READ
THINK
EXPLAIN

16 Ⓐ Ⓑ Ⓒ Ⓓ   **17** Ⓕ Ⓖ Ⓗ Ⓘ   **18** Ⓐ Ⓑ Ⓒ Ⓓ

19 Ⓕ Ⓖ Ⓗ Ⓘ

20

READ
THINK
EXPLAIN

21 Ⓐ Ⓑ Ⓒ Ⓓ   **22** Ⓕ Ⓖ Ⓗ Ⓘ

23 (A) (B) (C) (D) **24** (F) (G) (H) (I) **25** (A) (B) (C) (D)

26 (F) (G) (H) (I)

27
READ
THINK
EXPLAIN

28 (A) (B) (C) (D) **29** (F) (G) (H) (I) **30** (A) (B) (C) (D)

31
READ
THINK
EXPLAIN

32 Ⓕ Ⓖ Ⓗ Ⓘ

33

READ
THINK
EXPLAIN

_____
_____
_____
_____
_____
_____

34 Ⓐ Ⓑ Ⓒ Ⓓ   **35** Ⓕ Ⓖ Ⓗ Ⓘ   **36** Ⓐ Ⓑ Ⓒ Ⓓ

37 Ⓕ Ⓖ Ⓗ Ⓘ   **38** Ⓐ Ⓑ Ⓒ Ⓓ   **39** Ⓕ Ⓖ Ⓗ Ⓘ

40

READ
THINK
EXPLAIN

_____
_____
_____
_____
_____
_____
_____
_____
_____
_____
_____
_____

41 Ⓐ Ⓑ Ⓒ Ⓓ   **42** Ⓕ Ⓖ Ⓗ Ⓘ   **43** Ⓐ Ⓑ Ⓒ Ⓓ

44 Ⓕ Ⓖ Ⓗ Ⓘ

45

READ
THINK
EXPLAIN

46 Ⓐ Ⓑ Ⓒ Ⓓ   **47** Ⓕ Ⓖ Ⓗ Ⓘ   **48** Ⓐ Ⓑ Ⓒ Ⓓ

49

READ
THINK
EXPLAIN

50

READ
THINK
EXPLAIN

Practice Test 2 _____

Read the poem and then do Numbers 1 through 7.

LAUGHTERTOWN
by Katherine Devereux Blake

Oh, show me the road to Laughtertown,
For I have lost the way!
I wandered out of the path one day,
When my heart was broke and my hair turned gray,
And I can't remember how to play,
I've quite forgotten how to be gay;
It's all through sighing and weeping, they say.
Oh, show me the road to Laughtertown,
For I have lost the way!

I used to belong to Laughtertown,
Before I lost the way,
For I danced and laughed the livelong day,
Ere my heart was broke, and my hair turned gray;
So it ought to be easy to find the way!
But crying has made me blind, they say,
And still towards Teartown my sad feet stray.
Oh, show me the road to Laughtertown,
For I have lost the way!

Would ye learn the road to Laughtertown,
O ye who have lost the way?
Would ye have young hearts, though your hair be gray?
Go learn from a little child each day,
Go serve his wants and play his play,
And follow his dancing feet as they stray,
And catch the lilt of his laughter gay,
For he knows the road to Laughtertown,
O ye who have lost the way!

1 What is the poet's problem?

    A. Her children don't know how to dance.

    B. She is sad and doesn't know how to laugh.

    C. She is lost in a town which is new to her.

    D. She doesn't like to have fun.

2 How does the poet say this problem can be resolved?

    F. by crying more and more

    G. by taking lessons in smiling

    H. by copying children in play

    I. by going on a vacation

3 The title of the poem is "Laughtertown." What is "Laughtertown"?

    A. a city in Florida full of old people

    B. a place in the woods far from the city

    C. a theme park

    D. an imaginary happy place

4 What lesson does this poem teach?

    F. Only very young children should play and dance.

    G. Laughter isn't good for your health.

    H. Tears are one way to stay young.

    I. Adults can learn how to have fun from children.

5 Read this line.

> **And I can't remember how to *play*.**

Which sentence uses *play* in the same way as in the poem?

A. I fell in love with the *play* the first time I saw it.

B. Don't tell me you *play* with dolls.

C. They weren't fighting. They were *play* acting.

D. It's not real money. It's *play* money.

6 READ THINK EXPLAIN What does the poet feel about laughter? Give details and information from the poem in your answer?

7 Many poems by many authors are included in an

F. atlas.

G. anthology.

H. almanac.

I. autobiography.

Read this selection which was taken from *The People's Medical Manual*, by Howard and Martha Lewis. Then answer Numbers 8 through 14.

WATER SAFETY

TO RESCUE A DROWNING PERSON

Don't jump in to save a drowning person unless you are a trained lifesaver. The victim may pull you under.

Instead, try to toss a life preserver if you have one. Anything that will float can save the person's life. A beach ball, a vacuum jug, or a picnic chest will also help. The National Safety Council points out that many drownings could be prevented if people knew how many common objects float well enough to help a drowning person.

If you're in a boat, or you can find one, try to reach the person in a boat. Turn the boat so the victim can grab the stern (rear). Don't stand up to help the victim. Stay seated so the boat won't overturn. Try to balance the boat as the person climbs aboard. If the boat overturns, stay hanging on to the side for a while to relax before trying to right the boat.

DROWNPROOFING

1   2   3   4   5   6

SWIMMING PRECAUTIONS

To save your own life, practice "drownproofing." This is a technique for saving your strength in swimming emergencies. (See the diagram above.)

Instead of weighing you down in water, clothes—even heavy clothes—trap air and help you float. Clothes are buoyant in the water. Paddle to safety with a breast stroke. Allow most of your body to remain underwater. The more of your body you try to keep above water, the more energy you waste.

Overcome the urge to thrash about, which wastes energy and lets air escape.

If you get a cramp while swimming, draw your knees up to your chest while floating and massage the cramped muscle. Keep away from fast-moving water and watch out for under-water currents. If you are caught in a current, swim with it and at the same time, try to head toward shore.

Determine how deep water is before swimming or diving into it. Don't dive into unknown waters. Rocks or tree stumps may be concealed beneath the surface.

Avoid swimming alone—use the buddy system. This means that you must always have a swimming buddy and that each of you must keep track of where the other one is at all times. Don't swim at night except in lighted pools. Don't go swimming when tired. Don't dive into extremely cold water. The shock may cause muscle cramps. Staying for a long time in water below 65 degrees Fahrenheit can cause death from loss of body heat.

If you fall into cold water, avoid unnecessary thrashing about. Activity will drain the heat from your body. By floating as still as you can, you'll also keep air in your clothing, which helps to keep you warm and to keep you afloat.

Stay with an overturned boat instead of trying to swim a long distance to shore. If you can't right the boat, grasp the edge and kick-paddle toward shore. Don't exhaust yourself to the point of not being able to hang on to the boat.

Prevent Children from Drowning

Teach kids to swim early. Even very young children can learn with good instruction.

Youngsters shouldn't fear water, but it's worse to let them think they're unsinkable. Comments the National Safety Council: "A noseful of water while splashing in the tub is a good lesson for a little one. He'll learn that water can hurt him if he's not careful."

Never leave a small child alone in the tub. It takes only a few moments for an infant to drown in small amounts of water, so let the doorbell or telephone ring. Hang a sign, BATHING BABY—COME BACK LATER, on your front door to keep neighbors from dropping in at bath time.

Keep the bathroom door shut to keep out crawling infants and toddlers. Never let them play in the bathroom unwatched.

Always supervise children who are swimming and wading. Cover or drain pools that are not being used. Fill old wells that are not being used with earth.

8 Imagine you are out on the lake in a boat. You see a person calling for help in the water. You get to the victim in your boat. What should you do? Use details and information from the article in your answer.

9 Read this line.

Clothes are buoyant in the water.

When something is buoyant, it

A. drags you under.

B. makes you think.

C. keeps you afloat.

D. keeps your body warm.

10 Which is NOT true?

F. Small children should not play by themselves in the bathtub.

G. Children should learn to swim as young as possible.

H. Small children should fear water.

I. Even if children can swim, you should watch them.

11 Which of these statements would the authors agree with?

A. Only trained lifesavers should jump in to save a drowning person.

B. If your boat overturns, swim for shore immediately.

C. Remove your clothes immediately if you fall into the water.

D. Swimming at night is safe.

12 You want to learn more about swimming accidents. Which book would you consult?

    F. "Olympic Swimmers"

    G. "Safety in a Submarine"

    H. "Swimming Safety Rules"

    I. "The Ocean: A Vast Land"

13 In the diagram, Picture 1 is the same as Picture 6. Why is the same picture shown twice?

    A. It shows that the steps are all repeated.

    B. This is the hardest part of learn.

    C. The other steps are not as important.

    D. This step should be done twice in a row.

14 What advice would you give to the parents of young children regarding swimming safety? Use details and information from the article in your answer.

Read the stories about King Arthur and about the Lion and the Mouse and then answer Numbers 15 through 22.

KING ARTHUR

A great king ruled England. The king had a young son named Arthur and a wise advisor called Merlin. The king was ill and knew he would die soon. He wanted Arthur to become the new king, but Arthur was too young. The king was afraid that, after his death, an evil knight from a nearby country would kill Arthur and become the ruler of England.

Merlin told the king to send Arthur away until he was fully grown. Then Merlin made a plan. After the king died, Merlin plunged a sword deep into a huge stone. It was impossible to pull the sword out of the stone. Then Merlin put a sign on the stone. The sign said:

Whoever pulls this sword out of the stone
Shall be the new King of England.

Many men came from all over England to try to pull the sword out of the stone. They all failed. "There must be a reason we cannot succeed," one knight said. After many years, when Arthur was fully grown, he saw the sword deep in the stone. He reached over and pulled the sword out without any difficulty. When the people saw Arthur pull the sword free, they all began to cheer. Arthur became the new King of England. "You were the one this sword was meant for," said Merlin. Arthur was a wise and brave king who ruled England well and did many great deeds.

THE LION AND THE MOUSE

Once when a lion was asleep a little mouse began running up and down on his tail. This soon woke up the lion, who placed his huge paw upon the small mouse and opened his big jaws to swallow him.

"Forgive me, oh forgive me, O King," cried the little mouse who knew the lion liked to be called king because lions believe they are king of the jungle. "Forgive me this time and I shall never forget it. And who knows, one day you may need my help." The lion looked at the tiny mouse and laughed. "I, I would need the help of a little helpless mouse? Never!"

And the lion began to laugh again. He laughed and laughed and then said, "You made me feel happy today so I will let you go."

Months later, the lion was caught in a net by a hunter who wanted to bring him to the emperor of the land. Just then the little mouse happened to come by, and seeing the lion caught, began to chew on the net, which soon tore apart. After the lion was free, the mouse said, "Well?"

The lion smiled at the mouse and picked him up in his paw. "I am so glad you were right," he said.

Adapted from an Aesop Fable

15 Why did Merlin plunge the sword into the stone?

F.   to keep anyone from ever using the sword

G.   to keep the sword sharp

H.   so that no one would ever become ruler

I.   so that only Arthur would be king

16 Why did men try to pull the sword out of the stone?

    A. They wanted to be king.

    B. They thought the sword would make them wiser.

    C. They wanted to sell the sword.

    D. They thought the sword was very strong.

17 | READ THINK EXPLAIN | Why did the other men fail when they tried to pull out the sword?

18 Why did the lion want to eat the mouse?

    F. The lion was very hungry.

    G. The mouse was bothering him.

    H. The mouse wanted to be eaten.

    I. The lion only ate mice.

19 | READ THINK EXPLAIN | What does the lion mean when he says to the mouse, "I am so glad you were right?" Use details and information from the story in your answer

20 Why did the lion let the mouse go?

    A. The mouse made him happy.

    B. The mouse was too small to eat.

    C. The mouse escaped before he could eat him.

    D. The lion was scared and ran off.

21 The story "King Arthur" is a legend. The story "The Lion and the Mouse" is a fable. You can tell "The Lion and the Mouse" is a fable because

    F. The lion was asleep.

    G. The mouse was very small.

    H. The lion was caught.

    I. The animals talk.

22 What do these stories tell us about strength? Does the strongest person always succeed? Compare the strength of the lion with the strength of King Arthur. Use details and information from both stories.

This selection is about a remarkable flying creature that lived a long time ago. Read it and answer Numbers 23 through 29.

Have you ever heard of the flying reptile called Quetzalcoatlus? Can you even pronounce its name? It lived long ago, during the Age of Dinosaurs. It was the biggest flying animal that ever lived. Its wings measured 40 feet from tip to tip—as wide as the wings of a small airplane. Imagine looking up and seeing a creature like that soaring over your head! (And it's pronounced KWET-zal KWAT-luss.)

No bird has ever been as big as Quetzalcoatlus. The bird with the longest wings today, the albatross, has wings about 12 feet long when fully extended. The wings of Quetzalcoatlus were more than 3 times bigger. They were nearly as long as the entire body of the monster, meat-eating dinosaur, T. rex !

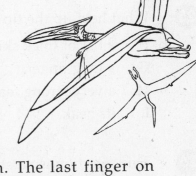

Quetzalcoatlus wasn't a bird. It was a reptile, like snakes, lizards, alligators, and dinosaurs. Birds have feathers. Quetzalcoatlus and its relatives didn't have feathers at all. Instead, they flew on wings made of very tough, thin skin. The last finger on Quetzalcoatlus' "hand" was as long as its whole arm. The skin that formed the wing stretched from the creature's side to its arm and wing finger.

What did Quetzalcoatlus eat? Many scientists believe it ate the bodies of dead dinosaurs. It may have looked for food while soaring in slow circles high in the air, hardly moving its wings at all. If it spotted a body that looked good enough to eat, it circled lower and lower, watching out for danger before it landed. This is the way the birds known as vultures or buzzards feed today.

These flying creatures are all gone now. They all died when the dinosaurs did. Earth may never again see a flying animal as big as the giants of 65 million years ago.

23 Read this sentence.

The bird with the longest wings today, the albatross, has wings about 12 feet long when fully *extended*.

The word *extended* means

A.   stretched out.

B.   very big.

C.   meat-eating.

D.   folded.

24 How did birds and Quetzalcoatlus compare? How were they different? Use details and information from the article in your answer.

25 What held up the tip end of the wing of a Quetzalcoatlus?

F.   a bar of thick skin.

G.   a long finger.

H.   a very strong feather.

I.   its beak.

26 This selection is mostly about

A.   a flying reptile.

B.   a giant bird.

C.   huge dinosaurs that lived a long time ago.

D.   what Quetzalcoatlus ate.

27 Which detail most supports the main idea?

    F.   Quetzalcoatlus didn't have feathers.

    G.   Quetzalcoatlus lived long ago.

    H.   Quetzalcoatlus may have eaten the bodies of dead dinosaurs.

    I.   The last finger on Quetzalcoatlus' "hand" was as long as its whole arm.

28 The author seems to feel that

    A.   Quetzalcoatlus was a marvelous creature.

    B.   Quetzalcoatlus was cruel and dangerous.

    C.   Quetzalcoatlus was really no different from hundreds of other animals.

    D.   Quetzalcoatlus was just like a bird.

29 What kind of airplane today flies most like a Quetzalcoatlus?

    F.   a fighter plane.

    G.   a helicopter.

    H.   a sailplane or glider.

    I.   a jet plane.

This selection is from the book *Where the Red Fern Grows* by Wilson Rawls. Read it and then answer Numbers 30 through 35.

The following spring we left the Ozarks. The day we moved I thought everyone would be sad, but it was just the opposite. Mama seemed to be the happiest one of all. I could hear her laughing and joking with my sisters as they packed things. She had a glow in her eyes I had never seen before and it made me feel good.

I even noticed a change in Papa. He didn't have that whipped look on his face any more. He was in high spirits as we carried the furniture out to our wagon.

After the last item was stored in the wagon, Papa helped Mama to the spring seat and we were ready to go.

"Papa, would you mind waiting a few minutes?" I asked. "I'd like to say good-bye to my dogs."

"Sure," he said, smiling. "We have plenty of time. Go right ahead."

Nearing the graves, I saw something different. It looked like a wild bush had grown up and practically covered the two little mounds. It made me angry to think that an old bush would dare grow so close to the graves. I took out my knife, intending to cut it down.

When I walked up close enough to see what it was, I sucked in a mouthful of air and stopped. I couldn't believe what I was seeing. There between the graves, a beautiful red fern had sprung up from the rich mountain soil. It was fully two feet tall and its long red leaves had reached out in rainbow arches curved over the graves of my dogs.

I had heard the old Indian legend about the red fern. How a little Indian boy and girl were lost in a blizzard and had frozen to death. In the spring, when they were found, a beautiful red fern had grown up between their two bodies. The story went on to say that only an angel could plant the seeds of a red fern, and that they never died; where one grew, that spot was sacred.

Remembering the meaning of the legend, I turned and started hollering for Mama.

"Mama! Mama!" I shouted. "Come here! And hurry! You won't believe it."

In a frightened voice, she shouted back, "What is it, Billy? Are you all right?"

"I'm all right, Mama," I shouted, "but hurry. You just won't believe it."

Holding her long skirt in her hand and with a frightened look on her face, Mama came puffing up the hillside. Close behind her came Papa and my sisters.

"What is it, Billy?" Mama asked, in a scared voice. "Are you all right?"

"Look!" I said, pointing at the red fern.

Staring wide-eyed, Mama gasped and covered her mouth with her hand. I heard her say, almost in a whisper, "Oh-h-h-h, it's a red fern—a sacred red fern." She walked over and very tenderly started fingering the long red leaves. In an awed voice, she said, "All my life I've wanted to see one. Now I have. It's almost unbelievable."

30 Before leaving, Billy wanted to visit

    A. a friend from school.

    B. the graves of his dogs.

    C. his old house.

    D. his school teacher.

31 Why was Billy's mother scared?

    F. Billy was yelling.

    G. The fern was very large.

    H. She was in danger.

    I. Billy's sister was hurt.

32 Why did Billy want to cut down the bush? Why did he change his mind? Use details and information from the story in your answer.

33 A legend is similar to

    A. a poem.

    B. a history.

    C. a myth.

    D. a children's story.

34 This story takes place

    F. in a wooded area.

    G. near the ocean.

    H. in a large city.

    I. in a desert.

35 Why was Billy's mother excited when she saw a red fern? Use details and information from the story in your answer.

Read this article and then answer Numbers 36 through 41.

A VISIT TO CONEY ISLAND

It's a hot summer Saturday in 1904, and it's going to get hotter. You and your family are riding a trolley (a streetcar that runs on overhead electric wires) in Brooklyn, New York. You are carrying your swimsuits, blankets, and picnic food. At the end of the line, you get off and see the sign: CONEY ISLAND. You can hardly contain your excitement at what you see, hear, and smell: the Boardwalk with its food stands serving hot dogs, cotton candy, and steamed clams, the roller coasters roaring along their tracks with screaming passengers, people jumping from the parachute tower, the carousels, and finally the beach where thousands are jammed, blanket to blanket, near the pounding waves.

Coney Island was "America's Playground" from 1884 to 1964. It was a place where the multitudes of people who worked hard at jobs in the hot, crowded city could come for a day of excitement, fun, and cool ocean breezes. Other nicknames for Coney Island were the "Nickel Empire," because almost all rides cost a nickel, and "The Poor Man's Paradise." The crowds were vast. More than 80,000 people might show up on a warm day. Coney Island became world famous. It was imitated all over the world by newer amusement parks, like Walt Disney World.

What made Coney Island so special? In the 1890s, it had one of the first Ferris wheels and a mechanical horse race on metal tracks called the Steeplechase. People could parachute from towers, whirl in a spinning drum, shoot a waterfall in a boat that ran on metal rails, and spin around the loop-the-loop. In 1903, Luna Park was added, with its gorgeous fake palaces, towers, lagoons, waterfalls, and walkways. It was lit by 250,000 electric lights, a startling sight to people of that time who were used to only gas lights. In another section, called Dreamland, they could watch a simulation of a volcano erupting or visit an African village of Somali warriors. They could watch a six-story building burn, while actors leaped into nets. No wonder Coney Island was a must-see tourist attraction of the time. Of course, all that has changed.

36 The Steeplechase was

A. a horse ride.

B. a water slide.

C. a parachute ride.

D. a rollercoaster.

37 Why was Coney Island called "The Poor Man's Paradise"?

F. It was always very crowded.

G. It was cheaply built.

H. Most of its rides and attractions cost only a nickel.

I. Rich people would never go there.

38 READ THINK EXPLAIN Why did people like to visit Coney Island? Use details and information from the article in your answer.

39 Read this sentence.

> In another section, called Dreamland, they could watch a *simulation* of a volcano erupting or visit an African village of Somali warriors.

Something that is a *simulation* is

A. an imitation.

B. badly made.

C. difficult to understand.

D. very large.

40 Pick out an opinion from the selection and tell why it is not a fact.

41 How does Coney Island Park compare with Walt Disney World?

F. Coney Island Park was harder to get into.

G. Coney Island Park was located in Miami.

H. Walt Disney World is smaller.

I. Walt Disney World is newer.

42 If you wanted to find out more about Coney Island, which book would you read?

A. "Tales of Strange Monsters"

B. "A History of Walt Disney World"

C. "The Earliest Theme Parks"

D. "New York City's Subway System"

Mrs. Lloyd has an interesting job. She makes gardens. Read the article and answer Numbers 43 through 50.

GREEN THUMB

SECTION 1

Mrs. Lloyd plants gardens all over Illinois. She makes gardens in the back of museums, next to big libraries, in hospitals, and even next to large office buildings. Her gardens always have plants of different colors, and she tries to arrange it so that some flowers are in bloom almost every month of the year.

SECTION 2

It's hard to choose the right plants for a garden. Most plants won't grow well unless they have the right soil or the right amount of water or the right amount of sun or shade. Mrs. Lloyd has a deep understanding of hundreds of plants, and she knows the conditions they like.

She says that when she started to work, in 1980, she visited gardens all over the Midwest at all times of the year, to see which flowers grew best. She had an unusual way to study the earth in the various gardens. She used to taste the soil. Actually, she would only put a little in her mouth to see if it was salty or bitter. When her daughter was in nursery school, she told the teacher that her mommy's job was to eat all the dirt, and this has been a family joke ever since.

But she doesn't ingest dirt anymore. Now she takes a small sample to the laboratory for analysis and a computer tells her all the plants that would grow best in that soil.

SECTION 3

She says that chemical analysis and computer charts are very effective, but she misses her old way of working.

43 What would you expect to find in one of Mrs. Lloyd's gardens in September?

    F.   all of the flowers in bloom

    G.   some of the flowers in bloom

    H.   no flowers in bloom

    I.   no flowers at all

44 The purpose of Section 1 is to

    A.   describe why computers are useful in planning gardens.

    B.   explain the meaning of the picture.

    C.   tell the reader how to select the best plants.

    D.   tell what Mrs. Lloyd does for a living.

45 Why has Mrs. Lloyd switched to using chemical analysis and computers?

    F.   Everyone in Illinois likes to use computers.

    G.   She didn't want her daughter to make fun of her.

    H.   She got sick from eating dirt.

    I.   The new ways work better.

46 It seems that Mrs. Lloyd

    A.   does not like to travel.

    B.   faces many problems with her daughter.

    C.   has a large garden near her home.

    D.   likes her work.

47 READ THINK EXPLAIN

At one time Mrs. Lloyd ate dirt. Why did she do this? Why did she stop? Use details and information from the article in your answer.

48 Which picture shows how Mrs. Lloyd tests soil today?

F.

H.

G.

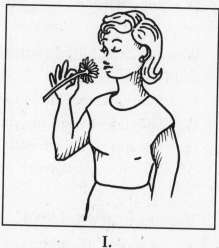

I.

49 In this story, the writer shows that

    A. everyone faces some difficulty in life.

    B. happiness doesn't come from success and money.

    C. people grow up, get married, and have children.

    D. people use new methods to do their jobs better.

50 The title of this story is "Green Thumb." Why is it named that?

    F. Mrs. Lloyd is good at growing flowers.

    G. Mrs. Lloyd likes to eat dirt.

    H. Mrs. Lloyd paints her thumb green.

    I. Mrs. Lloyd has a colorful personality.

Practice Test 2 Answer Sheet ———

1 Ⓐ Ⓑ Ⓒ Ⓓ   **2** Ⓕ Ⓖ Ⓗ Ⓘ   **3** Ⓐ Ⓑ Ⓒ Ⓓ

4 Ⓕ Ⓖ Ⓗ Ⓘ   **5** Ⓐ Ⓑ Ⓒ Ⓓ

6
READ
THINK
EXPLAIN
_____
_____
_____
_____
_____
_____

7 Ⓕ Ⓖ Ⓗ Ⓘ

8
READ
THINK
EXPLAIN
_____
_____
_____
_____
_____
_____

9 Ⓐ Ⓑ Ⓒ Ⓓ   **10** Ⓕ Ⓖ Ⓗ Ⓘ   **11** Ⓐ Ⓑ Ⓒ Ⓓ

12 Ⓕ Ⓖ Ⓗ Ⓘ   **13** Ⓐ Ⓑ Ⓒ Ⓓ

14

READ
THINK
EXPLAIN

15 Ⓕ Ⓖ Ⓗ Ⓘ   **16** Ⓐ Ⓑ Ⓒ Ⓓ

17

READ
THINK
EXPLAIN

18 Ⓕ Ⓖ Ⓗ Ⓘ

19

READ
THINK
EXPLAIN

20 Ⓐ Ⓑ Ⓒ Ⓓ   **21** Ⓕ Ⓖ Ⓗ Ⓘ

22

READ
THINK
EXPLAIN

23 Ⓐ Ⓑ Ⓒ Ⓓ

24

READ
THINK
EXPLAIN

_____
_____
_____
_____
_____
_____
_____

25 Ⓕ Ⓖ Ⓗ Ⓘ   **26** Ⓐ Ⓑ Ⓒ Ⓓ   **27** Ⓕ Ⓖ Ⓗ Ⓘ

28 Ⓐ Ⓑ Ⓒ Ⓓ   **29** Ⓕ Ⓖ Ⓗ Ⓘ

30 Ⓐ Ⓑ Ⓒ Ⓓ   **31** Ⓕ Ⓖ Ⓗ Ⓘ

32

READ
THINK
EXPLAIN

_____
_____
_____
_____
_____
_____

33 Ⓐ Ⓑ Ⓒ Ⓓ   **34** Ⓕ Ⓖ Ⓗ Ⓘ

35

READ
THINK
EXPLAIN

36 (A) (B) (C) (D)   **37** (F) (G) (H) (I)

38

READ
THINK
EXPLAIN

39 Ⓐ Ⓑ Ⓒ Ⓓ

40

READ
THINK
EXPLAIN

41 Ⓕ Ⓖ Ⓗ Ⓘ   **42** Ⓐ Ⓑ Ⓒ Ⓓ

43 Ⓕ Ⓖ Ⓗ Ⓘ   **44** Ⓐ Ⓑ Ⓒ Ⓓ   **45** Ⓕ Ⓖ Ⓗ Ⓘ

46 Ⓐ Ⓑ Ⓒ Ⓓ

47

READ
THINK
EXPLAIN

48 Ⓕ Ⓖ Ⓗ Ⓘ   **49** Ⓐ Ⓑ Ⓒ Ⓓ   **50** Ⓕ Ⓖ Ⓗ Ⓘ